So who is Robin Cooper?

Vinegar brewer, dartboard designer, octopus owner and champion bathtub polisher, Robin Cooper is all of these things, it just depends to whom he's writing . . .

Robin Cooper might also be the pseudonym for Robert Popper. Robert is a BAFTA-nominated writer and television producer, and co-creator and co-star of BBC2's hit comedy series, *Look Around You*. His first book, *The Timewaster Letters* was a bestseller.

Also by Robin Cooper

The Timewaster Letters

Return of the Timewaster Letters

ROBIN COOPER

TIME WARNER
BOOKS

TIME WARNER BOOKS

First published in Great Britain as a paperback original in
October 2005 by Time Warner Books

A CIP catalogue record for this book
is available from the British Library.

ISBN 0 316 73129 3

Typeset by M Rules
Printed and bound in Great Britain
by Clays Ltd, St Ives plc

Time Warner Books
An imprint of
Time Warner Book Group UK
Brettenham House
Lancaster Place
London WC2E 7EN

www.twbg.co.uk

Acknowledgements

*Severe thanks to the following, for helping me get this book
(that you are holding, or looking at whilst someone else is
holding) made:*

Simon Trewin
Tom Bromley
Sean Garrehy

Further severe thanks must also be offered to:

My parents, Jonny, Natalie (www.natalieshaw.com), Peter and
Sarah ('Hebbo again'), Tamsin Barrack, Cecilia Duraes, Simon
Henwood, the postman, CBD Research, everyone who kindly gave
me a quote, everyone who ever replied to my letters, and anyone
whose name should be on this list but isn't because someone else
forgot.

**Robin Cooper
Brondesbury Villas
London**

Prince Charles
The Prince of Wales
St James' Palace
London SW1A 1BS

26th May 1999

Dear Your Highness,

For years I have followed your comments on the state of British 'Architecture' with great interest. I share your views whole-heartedly, and feel, like you, that it is time to take a more Classical approach to the design of our public buildings.

You're a busy man, so I'll get straight to the point. I am a very keen amateur architect, and I believe that I have what it takes to become your own personal adviser on all things architectural.

You'll be pleased to know, Your Highness, that I don't ask for much, just a desk, some paper, a couple of pencils, and food and lodgings for my family.

But before you make your decision, please take time to view my latest designs (enclosed). They should give you a good idea of my worth as an architect.

The designs are for a new Dogs' Home. The idea came to me after my wife and I visited our local Dogs' Home last year. The building was in an awful state. On top of that, my wife broke a heel on a loose paving stone, and I was almost mauled to death by a manky old Collie!

So confident am I of my new appointment, that I shall be resigning from my present job in two weeks time.

I look forward to hearing from you with the good news – boss!

Your humble servant,

Robin Cooper

THE PRINCE OF WALES DOGS' HOME

Key

A Main Entrance

B1 Kitchen
B11 Bathroom
B111 Storeroom for dry and canned foods
B1a Luxury quarters for small pedigrees'
B1b Luxury quarters for large pedigrees'
B11a Standard kennel class for cross breeds (Holds up to 15 dogs per cell)
B11b Standard Kennel class (Same as B2a)
B11c Standard Kennel class (Same as B2b including toilets)
B11d Infected Breeds and ugly dogs
B11e Quarantine area (Foreign speaking dogs)
B11f Animal hospital (Including quarters for TV crews / Rolf Harris etc.)

C Dog Licence library

D Storage lockers for collars, identity tags, bells etc.

E Exercise run.

F Beauty centre for small pedigrees'

G Manure garden / K9 latrine

H All good dogs go to heaven (Graveyard and incinerator)

I Staff quarters

J Trained staff quarters

K11 Training pit
K111 Punishment area
K1V Cash point machine and mini mart
KV Puppy garden and Kitten annex

L Reception

M1 Empty room
M11 Empty room
M111 Empty room
M1V Empty room
MV Empty room
MV1 Empty room
MV11 Empty room
N Magnificent K9 Mosaic roof (Designed by Stephen Jiffer BA)

ST. JAMES'S PALACE
LONDON SW1A 1BS

From: The Office of HRH The Prince of Wales

8th June, 1999

Dear Mr. Cooper,

   The Prince of Wales has asked me to thank you for your letter of 26th May about your architectural requests.

   His Royal Highness is grateful to you for taking the trouble to write to him but regrets that he is unable to comply with your request. The Prince of Wales receives many letters every week asking for his assistance, but he simply cannot help on every occasion.

   His Royal Highness has asked me to send you his best wishes and trusts that your wife's ankle is mending.

Yours sincerely,

Miss Henrietta Rolston

Robin Cooper, Esq.

Robin Cooper
Brondesbury Villas
London

Prince Charles
The Prince of Wales
St James' Palace
London SW1A 1BS

16th June 1999

Dear Your Highness,

I received a reply to my previous letter (dated 26th May) on 8th June. It was sent to me - on your Royal Behalf - by Miss Henrietta Rolston.

Let me refresh your memory. I wrote to you regarding working as your Architectural Adviser, and I enclosed my design for 'The Prince of Wales Dogs' Home'. You may recall that I was going to resign from my job so that I could work for you.

Well, I did just that. Having worked for 19 years as a trampoline tester for Hilliard Gymnastics Supplies, I handed in my letter of resignation to Mr Hilliard himself. I told him where to stick his trampolines, and then proceeded to set fire to his waste paper basket. Even as I was turfed out onto the street, I felt like a million dollars because I knew that I would be working for you, My Highness.

Imagine my horror when I received a letter the very next day from your office, which stated, and I quote, "he (you) is (are) unable to comply with your (my) request"

Well thanks a lot! I am now out of work, and a laughing stock in the trampolining world.

My Lord, I beg you to reconsider - otherwise I face a life of wandering the streets, shouting at buses and eating rotten onions out of bin bags.

I look forward to a swift response and please can I have my designs back.

Your humble(d) servant,

R. Li Coy

Robin Cooper

PS – My wife's ankle is still in a bandage.

ST. JAMES'S PALACE
LONDON SW1A 1BS

From: The Office of HRH The Prince of Wales

2nd July, 1999

Dear Mr. Cooper,

The Prince of Wales has asked me to thank you for your further letter of 16th June.

Your reasons for writing as you did are appreciated, but I am sorry that you were disappointed by Henrietta Rolston's response. As she explained in her letter, most unfortunately it is not possible for His Royal Highness to offer you employment. You asked for your artwork to be returned and you will find it enclosed.

The Prince of Wales has asked me to send you his best wishes.

Yours sincerely,

Mrs. Hilton Holloway

Robin Cooper, Esq.

Robin Cooper
Brondesbury Villas
London

Prince Charles
The Prince of Wales
St James' Palace
London SW1A 1BS

17th August 1999

Dear Your Highness,

No doubt you recall me – I wrote to you on 16th June and also I wrote to you on 26th May in the year of Her Majesty 1999.

I, my Liege, was the man who gave up his job at Hilliard Gymnastics Supplies so that I could concentrate on becoming the Architectural Adviser to your Excellency, the Prince of Wales. You then wrote back and told me I couldn't work for you. As you know, I was distraught.

Let me give you an update on how things are going this end (I would ask you how you are but I read about you in the papers all the time so I know the answer). I managed to beg my old job back but have been forced to carry out petty and demeaning tasks as a kind of punishment and deterrent for others. Here is a breakdown of my day at work:

07:30 Clock in
07:40 Make tea for 18, coffee for 1 (Mr Hilliard)
08:20 Rinse cups
08:40 Clean staff cars (9)
11:00 Make coffee for 18, tea for 1 (Mr Hilliard)
11:30 Rinse cups
11:40 Polish and disinfect Mr Hilliard's telephone and chair
12:00 Empty bins
12:15 Declog sinks (6)
12:45 Take orders for lunch
13:15 Finish making sandwiches for staff
14:15 Clear away sandwiches and wipe surfaces. Bake cake for tea.
15:00 Hose down front steps, check for loose stones and repair
15:15 Check for pigeons and gulls nesting on roof. Remove.
15:45 Make tea for 18, coffee for 2 (Mr & Mrs Hilliard). Give out cake
16:25 Rinse cups and plates
17:00 Drive Mr & Mrs Hilliard home. Leave car at Mr Hilliard's.
18:30 Return to office by bus
18:35 Hoover premises, clear away office detritus
20:00 Take bus home.

Can you suggest a way out for me? Please reconsider using me as your Architectural Adviser. If you grant me the job, I will design you a new kitchen, the like of which you have never seen.

Please write back ASAP.

Your ever trustworthy servant,

Robin Co

Robin Cooper
PS – My wife is having her ankle x-rayed on the 25th August.

END OF CORRESPONDENCE

6

Robin Cooper
Brondesbury Villas
London

James Lomax
Chippendale Society
C/o Temple Newsam House
Leeds
W Yorks

29th July 1999

Dear James,

My wife is Chippendale mad! She's seen you and the lads do your act over FORTY times. Now that's got to be a record!

I thought it would be a nice surprise to send my wife a signed photo of the Chippendales for her birthday. Can you oblige?

Many thanks in advance (I've enclosed a SAE).

Yours sincerely,

[signature]

Robin Cooper

PS To be honest, I'm not so keen on my wife watching other men take their clothes off, but if it makes her happy, what can I do?

Robin Cooper
Brondesbury Villas
London

James Lomax
Chippendale Society
C/o Temple Newsam House
Leeds
W Yorks

16th August 1999

Dear James,

Hope you are well.

I wrote to you on 29th July requesting a signed photo of the lads 'in action' (letter included herewith).

I know you're a busy man what with all your shows, but if you could pop one in the post, it'll make my wife's day!

I look forward to hearing from you.

Yours sincerely,

R. L. C—

Robin Cooper

The Chippendale Society is devoted to Thomas Chippendale the furniture maker, not the Strippers!

END OF CORRESPONDENCE

Robin Cooper
Brondesbury Villas
London

Mr Simon Goldstein
Divisional Director
Menswear
Marks & Spencer Plc
Michael House
Baker Street
W1A 1DN

3rd August 1999

Dear Simon,

I am a young designer specialising in menswear. I have designed garments for such illustrious names as Prince Fauud, Lord Lingley, Darren Hardy and 'Pebbles', Taper Heverington, Thomas Dolby, Ploughter Hynan, and Richard and Margaret de Compte - to name but a few. I now have a new collection that I guarantee will BLOW YOUR MIND, and I'm sure will be an instant success for Marks & Spencer.

Would you be interested in seeing some of my designs? If so, I would be happy to send you my sketches.

I look forward to hearing from you.

Yours sincerely,

Robin Cooper

MARKS & SPENCER

REGISTERED OFFICE: MICHAEL HOUSE · BAKER STREET · LONDON WIA IDN
www.marks-and-spencer.co.uk

CHILDREN'S PROMISE
MILLENNIUM FINAL HOUR APPEAL

Mr R Cooper
Brondesbury Villas
London

9 August 1999

Dear Robin

Simon Goldstein has forwarded your letter onto me. If you would like to send me some of your sketches I would be happy to give you my views on them.

Yours sincerely

SIMON DAVY
Menswear Design Manager

StMichael

THE BRAND NAME OF MARKS AND SPENCER p.l.c.
REGISTERED NO. 214436 (ENGLAND AND WALES)

THE QUEEN'S AWARD FOR
EXPORT ACHIEVEMENT 1995 1997
THE QUEEN'S AWARD FOR
TECHNOLOGICAL ACHIEVEMENT 1996

10

Robin Cooper
Brondesbury Villas
London

Simon Davy
Menswear Design Manager
Marks & Spencer Plc
Michael House
Baker Street
W1A 1DN

10th August 1999

Dear Simon,

Hearty thanks for your letter in reply to mine which was sent (to Mr Simon Goldstein) on 3rd August.

You requested some of my designs, so please find attached a few of my latest sketches. These designs are part of my latest collection, entitled 'Scab'.

The inspiration behind 'Scab' comes from watching the blood congeal on an infected tortoise I once owned, named Sammy. Of course the clothes are designed with comfort primarily in mind and in keeping with the traditional values of Marks & Spencer's fashion.

Anyway, I hope you like the ideas and welcome your thoughts (and orders!).

I look forward to hearing from you.

Yours sincerely,

Robin Cooper

PS – Isn't it confusing having 2 Simons working in the same office?!

Scab

CLOTHES FOR MEN BY ROBIN COOPER
EXCLUSIVELY FOR MARKS + SPENCER

① <u>TROUSERS</u>

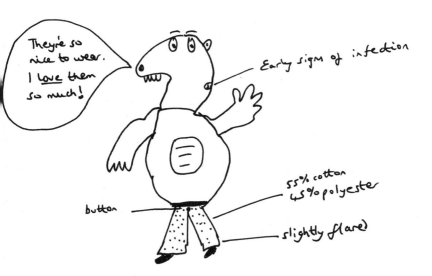

They're so nice to wear. I <u>love</u> them so much!

Early sign of infection

button

55% cotton 45% polyester

slightly flared

Available in red and blue (navy)

Sammy the tortoise <u>always</u> wears
'Scab' trousers...

£19.99

② <u>SHIRTS</u>

infection is spreading

nice collar

This shirt stops me from getting hot under the collar!

cigarette (not included)

cuffs

non-crease material (patented)

button

Available in white.

Sammy the tortoise never goes any~~way~~ where without his 'Scale' shirt on his 'back'!

sorry Simon

£ 15.99

13

③ HATS

Sammy the tortoise never leaves 'home' without wearing his favourite 'Scab' hat atop his funny, little head.

£10.99

END OF CORRESPONDENCE

14

Robin Cooper
Brondesbury Villas
London

Mr R French
Chief Executive
The Kennel Club
Clarges Street
London
W1Y 8AB

26th August 1999

Dear Mr French,

Woof woof!

Hope you like my little joke. Will you print it in your next newsletter?

I look forward to your response.

Keep up the good work.

Yours sincerely,

Robin Cooper

THE KENNEL CLUB
Chief Executive: Mr R. French

. ■ .

Clarges Street ▪ Piccadilly
London W1Y 8AB

31 August 1999

Mr Robin Cooper
Brondesbury Villas
London

Dear Mr Cooper,

I am at a loss for woofs and, quite frankly, do not understand your little joke!

Yours sincerely,

Roger French
Chief Executive (Secretary)

END OF CORRESPONDENCE

Robin Cooper
Brondesbury Villas
London

Jessica Alexander
Secretary
The Sleep Council
Chapel Hill
Skipton
N Yorks

15th December 1999

Dear Jessica,

I was fascinated to hear of your organisation, and wonder if you can help.

I am a very light sleeper and, on average, have about 3 hours sleep a night. Of late I have been told of a number of remedies which are meant to improve a night's sleep. Before I try them, I thought I would ask an expert (you) if any of them do actually work.

1) Place a dozen feathers under the pillow.
2) Put a bowl of sugar at the foot of the bed and a bowl of salt at the other end.
3) Lay 3 metres of aluminium foil under the bed.
4) Get a cat to breathe over you for half an hour.
5) Repeat the phrase 'Bim bim mim mim mim bim' one hundred times to oneself before getting undressed for bed.

Do any of these actually aid sleep?

I would be grateful if you could let me know.

Many thanks in advance.

Yours sincerely,

Robin Cooper

The Sleep Council

December 21, 1999

Mr R. Cooper
Brondesbury Villas
London

Dear Mr Cooper

Thank you for your letter. I must say I have never come across the sleep tips you mention beforehand and Have no means to judge their efficacy or otherwise. Being of a rather pragmatic nature, I'm afraid I am rather skeptical – although your last tip, with its association with meditation, could well help as it would help you to relax.

Yours sincerely

Jessica Alexander King Associates
for The Sleep Council

END OF CORRESPONDENCE

Robin Cooper
Brondesbury Villas
London

Leonard Cox
Honorary Secretary
The National Vegetable Society
Newmarket Road
Redcar

1st February 2000

Dear Mr Cox,

I wonder if you can help.

I recently had lunch with a friend, during which I tasted a most interesting vegetable. From what I recall, its name was 'sellery'. It was rather unusual, but nonetheless delicious.

I would very much like to procure some of this 'sellery' and would be most grateful if you could provide me with a list of stockists.

Many thanks,

Yours sincerely,

Robin Cooper

The National Vegetable Society

HON. SECRETARY:
L. Cox, FNVS
Newmarket Road
Redcar

Dear Mr Coopers,

CELERY is not easy to grow.

The majority of celery purchased at this time of the year is imported. However I send a list of the best celery seed supplies + their address, also a leaflet on how to grow your own.

Wishing you success.

END OF CORRESPONDENCE

18

Robin Cooper
Brondesbury Villas
London

Reverend Barrie Williams
The Society of King Charles the Martyr
Chubb Hill
Whitby
N Yorks

25th August 2000

Dear Reverend Barrie,

May fortune smile 'pon you.

I too am a keen fan of King Charles the Martyr.

I wonder if you would be gracious enough to receive a sweet poem I have penned in his glorious honour?

Best wishes,

Robin Cooper

2.9.2000.

Dear Robin,

Thank you for your letter last week. I should be very interested to receive your poem. It is quite some time since I saw any original poem inspired by King Charles.

I look forward to hearing from you.

Yours sincerely,

Barrie Williams.

Robin Cooper
Brondesbury Villas
London

Reverend Barrie Williams
The Society of King Charles the Martyr
Chubb Hill
Whitby
N Yorks

29th September 2000

Dear Barrie Williams,

I thank you for your response of 2nd September 2000 to my letter previous. Please accept my sincere apologies for the delay – I'm afraid I spent the last 3 weeks lost in Dartmoor after a hiking accident with my wife.

I send you a poem, penned in the honour of King Charles The Martyr. It is called 'Syllabub Sovereign'.

SYLLABUB SOVEREIGN (by Robin Cooper)

O Where ist thy king,
King Charles, the Martyr?
Is he in the pantry,
Or stables,
Or Kindom yonder?

No, he ist by thy cook,
Supping the fruit and the milk,
Of the syllabub.

The syllabub that resteth,
'Pon the regal table,
The regal table,
The regal table,
The regal table,
…Of the Lord.

I trust you are fond of my couplets and look forward to your response. I have 12 more poems, scribed in his (King Charles The Martyr)'s honour.

Best wishes,

Robin Cooper

Chubb Hill,
Whitby,
N. Yorks.

8.10.2000.

Dear Robin,

Thank you for your letter which came last week.

I was interested to read your poem <u>Syllabub Sovereign</u>. which I like, and which I will certainly commend for inclusion in <u>Church and King</u> (I did say, did I not, that I am no longer editor?)

I must check one point with you. Should the last line of stanza 1 read 'Or kingdom yonder?' or is it really 'kindom'?

I note you have written other poems in honour of the Royal Martyr. Let us see how we get on with this one, but I am sure that others will be of interest.

Best wishes,
Barrie Williams.

Robin Cooper
Brondesbury Villas
London

Reverend Barrie Williams
The Society of King Charles the Martyr
Chubb Hill
Whitby
N Yorks

12th October 2000

Dear Barrie Williams,

Many thanks for your letter of 8th October regarding my poem **Syllabub Sovereign**. I was delighted that it pleased you and would be more delighted still if you keep me informed as to when or whither it is included in 'Church and King'.

You asked about the last line of the first stanza and if it should have read 'kingdom' or 'kindom'. Good question. Well, I wrote 'kindom' when I should have wrote 'kingdom' but now that I have reread it, I've grown rather fond of 'kindom'. However, please feel free to change it to 'kindom'.

I have dug up another poem, transcribed in benefaction of the Glorious Martyr King. It is called **The Looking Glass King**.

THE LOOKING GLASS KING (by Robin Cooper)

The Looking Glass King,
Peered round and then in,
To the mirror of his soul,
Which was fashioned in tin.

"Youth, sweet youth,
Thou hadst left me all alone",
"Yes", came the reply,
"All alone, at home".

"But I am the master,
The master of this realm".
"I know", came the reflection,
It's thou that holdeth the healm".

"I do indeed",
Said the monarch, all perturbed,
"But thou artst the Martyr King,
Please do not be disturbed".

When darkness fell,
The looking glass turn'd black,
And the King, quite alone,
Fashioned hemp into a sack.

I trust that this pleases your mind's eye and look forward to your response. I have plenty more!

Best wishes,

Robin Cooper

END OF CORRESPONDENCE

23

Robin Cooper
Brondesbury Villas
London

Walter J Anzer
Secretary
The Vinegar Brewers' Federation
Castlereagh Street
London

25th August 2000

Dear Walter,

Greetings from one vinegar brewer to another!!!!!!!

Please can you assist? I recently made some home-made vinegar from some berries
I found growing in the garden.

I do not know whether the berries are edible to man, but the birds do seem to like them.

In your opinion, should I drink the vinegar?

Many thanks,

Best wishes,

Robin Cooper

VINEGAR BREWERS' FEDERATION

W H GRIERSON CHAIRMAN
PETTS WOOD
KENT

Robin Cooper
Brondesbury Villas
London

Dear Mr Cooper

Your letter addressed to Walter Anzer regarding the "Vinegar" you have made has been passed to me for reply.

I have to say at the outset that I definitely could not recommend that you use this vinegar for consumption as the origin is not known.

The fact that birds eat the berriers that you have used is no proof that they would not contain toxins which could well be harmful to humans. There are species that can devour such things as strychnine with no ill effects, but this is definitely not the case with the human body.

I am intrigued to know the process you used to obtain vinegar from berries. There are very few fruits that contain enough sugar to allow fermentation to take place and produce sufficient alcohol to enable the acetification of even a low strength vinegar.

Should you wish to discuss further please contact me at the above address.

I hope this has been of assistance.

Yours sincerely

W H GRIERSON.

Robin Cooper
Brondesbury Villas
London

Mr W H Grierson
Chairman
The Vinegar Brewers' Federation
Petts Wood
Kent

29th September 2000

Dear Mr Grierson,

Many thanks for your letter of…I cannot fill in the date as you missed it off! (we all do these things!!!).

Anyway, if you recall, you were interested to know how I produced my vinegar from berries found in the garden.

I have drawn a diagram depicting the process. I trust this will enlighten you and your peers.

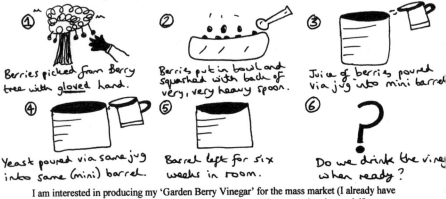

① Berries picked from Berry tree with gloved hand.

② Berries put in bowl and squashed with back of very, very heavy spoon.

③ Juice of berries poured via jug into mini barrel

④ Yeast poured via same jug into same (mini) barrel.

⑤ Barrel left for six weeks in room.

⑥ Do we drink the vinegar when ready?

I am interested in producing my 'Garden Berry Vinegar' for the mass market (I already have interest from Portugal). Is it OK for me to quote you on all the promotional material?

Keep up all the good work and I look forward to hearing from you.

Best wishes,

Robin Cooper

END OF CORRESPONDENCE

26

Robin Cooper
Brondesbury Villas
London

Dr Caroline Cahm
Chairman
The National Federation of Bus Users
PO Box 320
Portsmouth
Hants

26th April 2003

Dear Doctor,

I think congratulations are in order for being at the 'driving seat' of one of the finest bus-related organisations in the world.

I trust you will excuse my informality.

I have spent over 3 months designing a poster for the National Federation of Bus Users. This task helped me in my hour of need.

Can I send you the poster? It would mean a lot to me.

I await your reply with much anticipation.

With very best wishes,

Robin Cooper

NATIONAL FEDERATION OF BUS USERS

Chairman - Dr Caroline Cahm MBE, PhD, MCIT

2nd May 2003

Mr Robin Cooper
Brondesbury Villas,
LONDON

Dear Mr Cooper,

Thank you very much for your kind letter.

By all means send us the poster you have designed. However we use our own professionally designed poster and still have a big supply of these so shall not be able to consider using yours for the time being.

I enclose a leaflet about the National Federation of Bus Users as, since you have shown interest in our work, you may wish to become a member.

Yours sincerely,

Dr. Caroline Cahm, Chairman.

28

Robin Cooper
Brondesbury Villas
London

Dr Caroline Cahm
Chairman
The National Federation of Bus Users*
PO Box 320
Portsmouth

9th May 2003

Dear Doctor,

Thank you so much for your charming letter dated 2nd May.

I was absolutely delighted that you were interested in seeing my poster, which I have designed especially for your organization, the NFBU*. I therefore have great pleasure in enclosing my design, which I trust will interest you.

If you look carefully, you will notice that in the top left hand corner, I have included a drawing of the character 'Parmaynu'. Please do not be alarmed: the makers of Parmaynu, (Taylor Hemmol Ltd), have given me their complete backing and have agreed to Parmaynu becoming the face of the NFBU*. In return, all they have asked for is a small administrative charge of £1,400.

So confident am I that you will go with my campaign, that I have assured Taylor Hemmol that you will be able meet this cost.

I trust that this is in order, and that we can go ahead with my idea.

I look forward to hearing from you.

Best wishes and keep up the work!

1. li Coq

Robin Cooper

We simply could not afford this! I am very sorry
but your poster is not suitable for us.

CC

Dr C Cahm
chairm

29

'PARMAYNU,' THE PING PONG BAT [TM] SAYS:

" Whether you are a Professional, semi-pro, or amateur player,* you can <u>always</u> rely on one organisation: The **NFBU** – The NATIONAL FEDERATION OF <u>BUS</u> USERS. I should know – I'm an <u>expert</u> !!!"

* If you are an amateur table tennis player, there's nothing to be ashamed of – so use the bus!

© Robin Cooper 2003

END OF CORRESPONDENCE

Robin Cooper
Brondesbury Villas
London

The Reverend Granville Spedding
Vice Chairman
The Hover Club of Great Britain Ltd
PO Box 328
Bolton, Lancs.

17th May 2003

Dear Reverend,

I trust and hope that you are well.

Lord Poynton, (a friend of the family who I believe you know), mentioned that your organisation develops lightweight hovercraft for both sport and recreational use. This, he (Lord Poynton) did (mentioned), because of my interest in them (hovercrafts).

Am I therefore glad to have found you!?!

I have been working on a design for a new hovercraft for about 4 years, and have just completed a prototype. I believe that it is lighter and easier to use than any other hovercraft previous.

I have named the machine 'THE AIRSHIP HATH NO DISREGARD FOR NATURE 109', and I plan to test it on Salisbury Plain in September.

QUESTIONS:

1) Can I send you my designs?
2) I have painted your organisation's name and number along the flank. Is this OK?
3) Will you be there (Salisbury Plain)?
4) Should I test the device with a live, human driver, or a guinea pig (i.e. wolf?)

I look forward to hearing from you,

With very best wishes, and keep up the good work,

Robin Cooper

Cc Lord Poynton

Hovercraft Club of Great Britain

The National Organisation for Light Hovercraft

The Rev'd W Granville Spedding
HCGB Ltd., PO Box 328, Bolton, BL6 4FP
Vice Chairman Hovercraft Club: Secretary North West Branch: Information Officer: Publication & Sales.

1st June 2003

Robin Cooper
Brondesbury Villas,
London

Dear Robin

Your letter sound rather intriguing – though the reason for the name of your hovercraft is rather mystifying to say the least!

The machines that the Hovercraft Club regulates are used for both racing and recreation purposes. Races take place up and down the country at various venues throughout the summer – last weekend was at Fawley near Southampton, and the one I organise in the North West will take place at Tatton Park in Cheshire in September.

Cruising (recreation) hovercraft usually enjoy coastal events, the first being at Hunstanton, then on the River Severn, and finally in September at Abersoch, North Wales.

I would be delighted to see your designs, but we would prefer you not to include the club logo or other information till we have viewed your craft. We only want to be identified with craft that would be of the standard required by our regulations – anything less might be damaging to the professional image of the Hovercraft Club, identify you with the club as a member, (which I presume you are not at present) which could be misleading to observers and really should only be displayed by members of the club

It will not be possible for me to be on Salisbury plain in September – rather a long way from Lancashire – but if your trials are a serious attempt at producing something different in the design of hovercraft, then no doubt somebody might be persuaded to see what you have produced.

I cannot advise as to who should drive the craft – it is usually the inventor, unless he/she has little faith in the machine and would prefer someone else to take the risk to life and limb!

So I look forward to see you plans and photos, and may be seeing the trials of your hovercraft.

Finally, I am not sure how I know Lord Poynton; perhaps you could give me some more information about this.

With kind regards,

W Granville Spedding (Re)

Robin Cooper
Brondesbury Villas
London

The Reverend Granville Spedding
Vice Chairman
The Hover Club of Great Britain Ltd
PO Box 328
Bolton, Lancs.

4th June 2003

Dear Reverend,

I was truly honoured to receive a reply (1st June) to my letter (17th May). In response, I will follow my original numbering for ease of reference:

1) I was delighted that you were interested in seeing designs for my hovercraft, THE AIRSHIP HATH NO DISREGARD FOR NATURE 109 (enclosed). Please do excuse my rather poor draftsmanship - my wife has a terrible ankle and it has, alas, rather affected me.

As to the name of the beast (!), that's simple to solve. My cousin Alexander was travelling in Romania several years ago (having been made bankrupt - heaven knows how he afforded the trip) when he came across a filthy, old female beggar who had the words 'MIN TARPETA HULJ' printed across her forehead and arms. When Alex enquired as to what these words meant, the poor wretch replied, "The airship hath no disregard for nature". As for the '109' bit at the end, I don't know why I added that really.

2) You asked me to remove your organisation's name from my hovercraft, which I will of course do. May I go ahead and paint your initials ('WGS') on the machine instead? I was hoping to do each letter in a different colour and font. It would bring me great pleasure.

3) 'tis indeed a shame that you won't be at Salisbury Plain in September. You will miss the celebrated Louis de Cannet and his 'Show of Penance'. Are you sure you won't change your mind?

4) Regarding test driving the device, I will follow your advice and test drive THE AIRSHIP HATH NO DISREGARD FOR NATURE 109 myself. I hope I don't crash!!

As for Lord Poynton, he asked me to mention the phrase "never mind the washing up" to you. He said you would understand and that this would jog memories. He also wanted to know if you would return "the Canbury tiles"?

In the meantime I thank you for your time. I look forward to hearing from you regarding my design and am of course happy to pass on your reply to Lord Poynton.

Best wishes,

Robin Cooper
Cc Lord Poynton

Robin Cooper's Hovercraft *

Fan

Exhaust

Large waterproof Box

Air buffer (60% rubber 40% tenuin)

The Airship Hath NO Disregard For Nature 109

Seats

Emergency rubber ring

Clip
cord to hold rubber ring

bolt to secure rubber ring to craft

First aid Box affixed to Delp System

Pipe

Man

Throttle

Cartesic valve

'Info' screen

Your initials (different fonts)

WgS

Homing device (Calvin#6)

Water

mini lights

* The Airship Hath No Disregard For Nature 109
Top Speed: You decide !!!

END OF CORRESPONDENCE

34

Robin Cooper
Brondesbury Villas
London

Jeff Travis
Chief Executive
The Life Insurance Association
Station Approach
Chorleywood
Rickmansworth
Herts

17th December 2003

Dear Mr Travis,

Merry Christmas!

I wonder if you can help: my wife and I have a question regarding life insurance, and we have been advised by both Lord Telmer and Lady Pelving that you may be of assistance.

What are the precise stipulations regarding life insurance whereby a signatory A (a) and a signatory B (b) deign that a third party (iii) should be covered for and against any impropriety relating to *corpus immentus* or *sanguines polaris*, and would (b) be advised to reduce his (or her) premiums by transferral of equity via a non-recouperable transaction, given that (a) would be forced to admit *indemnus advocares* on account of (iiii) being absent at the time?

I thank you in advance for your help, and look forward to hearing from you.

Kindest regards,

Robin Cooper

Cc Lord Telmer
Lady Pelving

THE ASSOCIATION FOR FINANCIAL SERVICES PROFESSIONALS

27 January 2004

Mr Robin Cooper
Brondesbury Villas
LONDON

Dear Mr Cooper

I have a copy of a letter you sent to Mr Travis on 17 December 2003 in which you raise some issues regarding life assurance.

I am afraid the Latin terms you use in the letter are not readily accessible by legal advisers we have approached and it would be helpful if you could explain exactly the point of the enquiry and also the involvement of Lord Telmer and Lady Pelving who are unknown to us.

You will of course gather that Mr Travis is no longer chief executive of the LIA and we will in his absence, do our best to answer your enquiry if you could clarify the issues involved.

I am sorry it has taken some time to get back to you. I have been undertaking some research without, as I indicated, a great deal of success.

Yours sincerely

John Ellis
Head of Public Affairs

LIA House, Chorleywood, Rickmansworth, Hertfordshire

Increasing the competence, standing and success of our members

Robin Cooper
Brondesbury Villas
London

John Ellis
Head of Public Affairs
The Life Insurance Association
Station Approach
Chorleywood
Rickmansworth
Herts

28th Jaunary 2004

Dear Mr Ellis,

Many thanks for your kind letter of 27th January. I appreciate fully your response (to me).

You enquired as to the 'Latin' phrases in my previous correspondence. The phrases I used were actually written in 'Apple Latin', a form of Latin that was taught at my school. Apple Latin involves much swapping of vowels and consonances, switching of tenses, and a rather unique grammatical system. It was primarily used by generals and commanders at times of battle, when, presumably they did not want their adversaries to decipher their orders. I apologise for the confusion.

You also asked after Lord Telmer and Lady Pelving. Again I apologise for the confusion, as both names are actually pseudonyms. In the meantime, both have been consulted, and have decided to no longer be involved in this matter.

I do hope this has cleared things up a little.

Can you help?

I enclose a SAE for your troubles.

Many thanks again,

Best wishes,

[signature]

Robin Cooper

END OF CORRESPONDENCE

37

Robin Cooper
Brondesbury Villas
London

Dr Ad Needham
The Linguistics Association of Great Britain
Department of Phonetics & Linguistics
University College London
Gower Street
London WC1E 6BT

7th January 2004

Dear Doctor,

Tamparsyam.

Min maynu, jin-hardim metahaynu pavaysh. Henty henty swilby petarnu. Ralvim thalf futhum mim maynu?

I look forward to hearing from you.

Best wishes,

Robin Cooper

38

Robin Cooper
Brondesbury Villas
London

Mr R H Sinclair
General Secretary
The English Table Tennis Association
Havelock Road
Hastings
E Sussex

7th January 2004

Dear Mr Sinclair,

Allow me to begin by telling you just some of the fine things said (to me) of your wonderful organisation:

"The finest association around"
    Mr T Gates, Lincoln

"Always helpful. ALWAYS helpful"
    Ms Archer, Address withheld

"Fantastic!"
    Name and address withheld

Congratulations! I, I am sure, like your good self, am a table tennis nut! I play for about 4 hours every day of the week, every month of the year (except November), every year! I just love it. It's such a wonderful little game, don't you think?

Anyway, the reason I am writing is that I have designed a new range of table tennis bats bearing your association's name. Would you care to see them, before I go into production? I am pretty sure you will like them and give me the go ahead. I am planning on producing about 30,000.

Happy playing!

Best wishes,

Robin Cooper

Robin Cooper

39

English Table Tennis Associatio

(Affiliated to the ITTF and the ETTU)
Patron: HER MAJESTY THE QUEEN
President: JOHNNY LEACH, MBE

Ref: 61/RHS/LS

23rd January 2004

Mr R. Cooper
Brondesbury Villas
London

Dear Mr Cooper,

Thank you for your letter dated 7th January 2004.

The Association is very interested to see samples of the new range of table tennis bats you have designed and would ask you to telephone us on the number below to arrange a suitable date for a meeting.

We look forward to hearing from you.

Yours sincerely,

L Shipp

Lindsay Shipp
Secretary to Rob Sinclair
(General Secretary)

English Table Tennis Association Limited

Supported by

SPORT ENGLAND

Directors: ALEX MURDOCH (Chairman), MIKE JOHNS (Deputy Chairman), MARTIN CLARK (Treasurer).
Company Secretary: RICHARD YULE (Chief Executive) Registered in England and Wales No. 4268058

***SPORTING EQUALS** WORKING FOR RACIAL EQUALITY IN SPORT*

40

Robin Cooper
Brondesbury Villas
London

Lindsay Shipp
Secretary to Rob Sinclair
The English Table Tennis Association
Havelock Road
Hastings
E Sussex

28th January 2004

Dear Lindsay,

Many thanks for your charming letter of 23rd January in response to mine of the 7th January.

I was delighted that your association is interested in my new range of table tennis bats bearing your name (not yours personally – the association's!!).

I was also delighted that you were keen to set up a meeting at your premises. However I am sadly unable to travel to Hastings at present, due to a mixture of personal and religious reasons.

In the meantime, would you be interested in seeing some of the designs bearing your (we won't start that joke again!) name?

I look forward to hearing from you.

Happy playing!

Best wishes,

Robin Cooper

41

English Table Tennis Association

(Affiliated to the ITTF and the ETTU)
Patron: HER MAJESTY THE QUEEN
President: JOHNNY LEACH, MBE

Ref: 61/RHS/LS

29th January 2004

Mr R. Cooper
Brondesbury Villas
London

Dear Robin,

Re: Table tennis bats

Thank you for your letter dated 28th January 2004.

We would very much like to see some of your designs bearing our Association's name with the hope of arranging a meeting with you at our office in Hastings in the near future.

We look forward to receiving your designs.

Yours sincerely,

L. Shipp

Lindsay Shipp
Secretary to Rob Sinclair
(General Secretary)

English Table Tennis Association Limited

Supported by

**SPORT
ENGLAND**

Directors: ALEX MURDOCH (Chairman), MIKE JOHNS (Deputy Chairman), MARTIN CLARK (Treasurer).
Company Secretary: RICHARD YULE (Chief Executive) Registered in England and Wales No. 4268058

SPORTING EQUALS WORKING FOR RACIAL EQUALITY IN SPORT

42

Robin Cooper
Brondesbury Villas
London

Lindsay Shipp
Secretary to Rob Sinclair
The English Table Tennis Association
Havelock Road
Hastings
E Sussex

2nd February 2004

Dear Lindsay,

Many thanks for your delightful letter of 29th January, following my letter of the day previous. It seems we've almost been playing a game of 'Royal Mail ping pong'!

As promised, I now have the pleasure of unveiling some of my table tennis bat designs. You will notice that I have based my designs on the character of 'Parmaynu'. I have chosen Parmaynu, as I believe he represents everything good and wholesome about the game of ping pong. I trust you will agree.

Anyway, I look forward to your comments and trust that you will be keen for me to mass produce my 'Parmaynu Ping Pong Bats'.

With very best wishes,

Robin Cooper

Table Tennis Bats by Robin Cooper

All Featuring Parmaynu (TM)

1. 'The Patriot'

4. 'The Buccaneer'

2. 'The Pipe-Smoker'

5. 'Measles'

3. 'The Neapolitan'

6. 'Fitz'

44

Robin Cooper
Brondesbury Villas
London

Lindsay Shipp
Secretary to Rob Sinclair
The English Table Tennis Association
Havelock Road
Hastings
E Sussex

20th February 2004

Dear Lindsay,

I trust that you are well.

I wonder if you had the chance to peruse my 'Parmaynu Ping Pong bat' designs, that I sent to you on the 2nd February?

I do look forward to hearing from you.

Happy playing!

With very best wishes,

Robin Cooper

English Table Tennis Association

(Affiliated to the ITTF and the ETTU)
Patron: HER MAJESTY THE QUEEN
President: JOHNNY LEACH, MBE

Ref: 61/RHS/LS

25th February 2004

Mr R. Cooper
Brondesbury Villas
London

Dear Robin,

Re: Table tennis bats

Thank you for your letter dated 20th February 2004.

The Chief Executive and General Secretary of the Association have perused your 'Parmaynu ping pong bat' designs and would very much like to meet with you at our office in Hastings to discuss the matter further.

We await hearing from you to arrange a convenient date for a meeting.

Yours sincerely,

L. Shipp

Lindsay Shipp
Secretary to Rob Sinclair
(General Secretary)

English Table Tennis Association Limited

Supported by

SPORT ENGLAND

Directors: ALEX MURDOCH (Chairman), MIKE JOHNS (Deputy Chairman), MARTIN CLARK (Treasurer).
Company Secretary: RICHARD YULE (Chief Executive) Registered in England and Wales No. 4268058

SPORTING EQUALS WORKING FOR RACIAL EQUALITY IN SPORT

46

Robin Cooper
Brondesbury Villas
London

Lindsay Shipp
Secretary to Rob Sinclair
The English Table Tennis Association
Havelock Road
Hastings
E Sussex

2nd March 2004

Dear Lindsay,

Many thanks as ever for your lovely letter of 25th February regarding my 'Parmaynu Ping Pong bats'.

I was most excited to learn that both the Chief Executive and General Secretary of the Association enjoyed perusing my designs, and having discussed the matter with my wife, I would be delighted to travel up (or is it down?!!!) to Hastings for a meeting.

I am free from 8th March onwards, anytime during office hours (except Thursday 11th as my wife has a hospital appointment).

Please write back to confirm a suitable time.

I look forward to hearing from you.

Best wishes,

Happy playing!

Robin Cooper

English Table Tennis Association

(Affiliated to the ITTF and the ETTU)
Patron: HER MAJESTY THE QUEEN
President: JOHNNY LEACH, MBE

Our Ref: MLK/0013

26th March 2004

Mr R. Cooper
Brondesbury Villas
London

Dear Mr Cooper

With reference to your visiting our offices in Hastings to discuss the designs of your Parmaynu Ping Pong bats, I would be grateful if you could telephone me on the above number to arrange a mutually convenient date.

We look forward to hearing from you.

Yours sincerely

M L Knight
Secretary to General Secretary

Supported by

SPORT ENGLAND

English Table Tennis Association Limited

Directors: ALEX MURDOCH (Chairman), MIKE JOHNS (Deputy Chairman), MARTIN CLARK (Treasurer).
Company Secretary: RICHARD YULE (Chief Executive) Registered in England and Wales No. 4268058

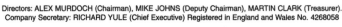

SPORTING EQUALS WORKING FOR RACIAL EQUALITY IN SPORT

48

Robin Cooper
Brondesbury Villas
London

M L Knight
Secretary to General Secretary
The English Table Tennis Association
Havelock Road
Hastings
E Sussex

30th March 2004

Dear Mr M L Knight,

Many thanks for your letter of 26th March regarding our planned meeting to discuss my 'Parmaynu Ping Pong bats'.

Sadly I am unable to use the telephone at present and thus cannot call you but I am available to come to your offices in Hastings on the following dates:

Monday 12th April – All day
Tuesday 13th April – All day
Wednesday 14th April – All day

Etc. etc until Wednesday 2nd June, as my wife is back in hospital for another X-ray on her wretched ankle. However this pattern would then continue from Thursday 3rd June, pretty much until Christmas (25th December).

In other words, I'm pretty FREE in general!

I look forward to confirming our meeting.

Happy playing!

Robin Cooper

15th April 2004
61/RHS/mlk-0074

English Table Tennis Association
(Affiliated to the ITTF and the ETTU)
Patron: HER MAJESTY THE QUEEN
President: JOHNNY LEACH, MBE

Mr Robin Cooper
Brondesbury Villas
London

Dear Mr Cooper

Thank you for your letter dated 30th March 2004.

Looking through the diary of Mr R Sinclair, it would seem that both Wednesday 28th April and 5th May would be equally suitable for a visit by your goodself. I will leave the time of arrival to you; just let us know when you confirm the date.

I look forward to hearing from you.

Yours sincerely

Mrs M L Knight
Secretary to General Secretary

English Table Tennis Association Limited

Supported by
SPORT ENGLAND

Directors: ALEX MURDOCH (Chairman), MIKE JOHNS (Deputy Chairman), MARTIN CLARK (Treasurer).
Company Secretary: RICHARD YULE (Chief Executive) Registered in England and Wales No. 4268058

SPORTING EQUALS WORKING FOR RACIAL EQUALITY IN SPORT

50

**Robin Cooper
Brondesbury Villas
London**

Mrs M L Knight
Secretary to General Secretary
The English Table Tennis Association
Havelock Road
Hastings
E Sussex

16th April 2004

Dear Mrs M L Knight,

I hope you are well.

Firstly, please allow me to apologise deeply for addressing you (in my previous letter), as 'Mr M L Knight'. It was an assumption I should never have made and I do, once again, apologise from the bottom of my heart, to you - Mrs M L Knight.

That said, (phew – that was one of the most difficult things I have ever had to write), I would be delighted to meet Mr R Sinclair to discuss my 'Parmaynu Ping Pong bats', in the comfort of your premises.

I am able to make a meeting on 5th May at 3:00pm. I shall be driving down with my wife, who will direct me during our journey.

I trust it would be OK if my wife could wait in reception during our meeting. My wife does have a bad ankle at the moment, so some form of padded footrest would be most appreciated.

In the meantime, I look forward to seeing you all, and to you say I say this:

Happy playing!

Robin Cooper

51

Robin Cooper
Brondesbury Villas
London

Mrs M L Knight
Secretary to General Secretary
The English Table Tennis Association
Havelock Road
Hastings
E Sussex

10th May 2004

Dear Mrs M L Knight,

I must begin this letter with a deep, humble apology.

As you know, we had arranged a meeting between our good selves (including Mr R Sinclair), at your premises on 5th May at 3:00pm.

My wife and I had made all the necessary preparations for the long journey ahead: the car's oil and water levels had been checked, as well as the tyres. Sandwiches had been prepared, along with sufficient water and gaseous drinks. However, just as my wife was lowering herself into the car, she trod on a piece of plastic wrapping (part of an old shampoo bottle), and re-sprained her ankle.

Thus we had to go straight to hospital. Alas, we never made our meeting. 'twas a fateful day…

I cannot apologise enough for our dismeneanour, and so, by way of recompense, am enclosing £5. I trust that this goes towards the price of a meeting room.

Best wishes,

Robin Cooper

Ref: 61/mlk0165

English Table Tennis Association

(Affiliated to the ITTF and the ETTU)
Patron: HER MAJESTY THE QUEEN
President: JOHNNY LEACH, MBE

11th May 2004

Mr Robin Cooper
Brondesbury Villas
London

Dear Mr Cooper

Thank you for your letter of the 10th May explaining the circumstances on the 5th May which hindered your making the meeting.

I do hope that your wife is recovering sufficiently to enable you to make another appointment. To this end I would like to offer you Wednesday 26th May or Wednesday 16th June at 3 p.m.

Your contribution of £5.00 was unexpected but most welcome and I thank you for this.

I hope to hear from you in the not too distant future.

Yours sincerely

Marie Knight

Marie Knight
Secretary to Robert Sinclair – General Secretary

English Table Tennis Association Limited

Supported by

**SPORT
ENGLAND**

Directors: ALEX MURDOCH (Chairman), MIKE JOHNS (Deputy Chairman), MARTIN CLARK (Treasurer).
Company Secretary: RICHARD YULE (Chief Executive) Registered in England and Wales No. 4268058

SPORTING EQUALS WORKING FOR RACIAL EQUALITY IN SPORT

Robin Cooper
Brondesbury Villas
London

Marie Knight
Secretary to General Secretary
The English Table Tennis Association
Havelock Road
Hastings
E Sussex

25th May 2004

Dear Marie,

Many thanks for your letter of 11th May. I do apologise for the tardiness of my reply. I am afraid that I only received your letter this morning. I can therefore assume two things:

1) The letter got mislaid in the system
2) Something else occurred untoward (but not on your behalf, I should add)

Nevertheless, I am glad you received my donation of £5. I do hope you have put it to good use.

Sadly, I am unable to make the meeting on the 26th, as this is now tomorrow! (Tomorrow for me, but by the time you get this letter, it will probably be yesterday for you, unless of course the above points 1 and 2 re-occur, which may mean this letter is a fortnight old – for you!).

I am also unable to make the 16th June, as I have an appointment with a persimologist, which I cannot change.

Perhaps we could re-arrange, or would you all be prepared to meet me at my Summer house in the New Forest?

I look forward to hearing from you.

I enclose a SAE, as a mark of respect.

Best wishes,

Robin Cooper

END OF CORRESPONDENCE

54

Robin Cooper
Brondesbury Villas
London

Keith Dunkinson
Chairman
The British Octopus Association
Ash Close
Northants
N11 5XH

16th February 2004

Dear Mr Dunkinson,

I heard about your organisation from the zoo.

I wonder if you would be so kind as to help.

I have recently acquired an octopus, which I keep in a water tank in my garage. The garage is well-ventilated and pretty clean, albeit slightly cluttered, (my wife keeps her ankle bandages here, along with her ointments), but in general is quite a good place to keep such a creature.

However, I do have a number of questions I would like to ask of you. I trust you do not mind.

1) How often should I change Raffety's water? (Raffety is the name of my octopus).
2) Is it OK to give Raffety biscuits every now and then, as 'treats'?
3) How often should Raffety be sleeping? At present it is roughly 23 hours a day.
4) Is it possible to teach octipi tricks (such as swimming through hoops etc.)? I would be keen to enter him into aquatic shows.

Many thanks in advance for your help.

I look forward to hearing from you,

With very best wishes,

Robin Cooper

BRITISH OCTOPUSH ASSOCIATION

The Controlling Body of Underwater Hockey in the United Kingdom

OCTOPUSH Is A SWIMMING SPORT.

I can't help Rafferty.

Regards

Karl.

END OF CORRESPONDENCE

Robin Cooper
Brondesbury Villas
London

The Manager
Claridge's
Brook Street
Mayfair
London W1A 2JQ

23rd February 2004

Dear Sir/Madam,

It has always been my dream to stay at Claridge's. Now I hope my dream can be fulfilled.

I am planning a weekend in your delightful hotel some time later in the year. However, since my requirements are a little 'special', I have a number of questions to ask you before I make my booking.

1) Would it be possible for all members of staff to address me as 'The Lizard' between the hours of 9-11am, 'The Captain' between 11:01-14:00, 'Godfrey Taylor' between 14:01-16:00 and 'The Lizard' again until I go to bed?

2) I am very particular about personal safety and would like you to test the fire alarm at least three times during my stay, with the full evacuation of all residents. Can this be done?

3) Could you organise three pales of blue ink to be left standing in the bath upon my arrival?

4) I shall be arriving with a fully automated robot calf. Can you arrange quarters?

I trust that these demands are not beyond your capabilities, and I look forward to your response.

With very best wishes.

Yours sincerely,

Robin Cooper

Claridge's

CC/pam

24th February, 2004

Mr. R. Cooper,
Brondesbury Villas,
London

Dear Mr. Cooper,

Thank you for your letter dated 23rd February, 2004.

Mr. Cooper, whilst we pride ourselves on endeavouring to meet our guests' special and, sometimes, unusual requests, I very much regret to advise that it would not be possible for us to fulfil the four requests contained within your letter.

We do hope that we will still have the pleasure of welcoming you to Claridge's and we look forward to your contacting us if you feel we can be of any further assistance to you.

Yours sincerely,

Christopher Cowdray
<u>MANGING DIRECTOR</u>

**Robin Cooper
Brondesbury Villas
London**

Christopher Cowdray
Managing Director
Claridge's
Brook Street
Mayfair
London W1A 2JQ

2nd March 2004

Dear Mr Cowdray,

Many thanks for your swift response to my letter which detailed my 'special' requests.

OK, I am willing to drop 3 of the 4 requests as I am so keen on staying in your hotel. However, I would like to keep point 4.

If you recall, point 4 related to the fact that I would like to bring along a fully automated robot calf. It travels everywhere with me, and I would beg you to let me take it (into your establishment). (Claridge's).

I am prepared to let the robot calf stay in my bedroom, but would need a member of staff to accompany the 'unit' at all times, as it has been known to malfunction.

For your convenience, I enclose a detailed drawing of the robot calf:

Eye

Aerial

Tiny Wheels

Cable (up to 90ft long, attached to mains socket).

I await your reply, and thank you in advance for your good faith.

Yours sincerely,

Robin Cooper

Claridge's

CC/pam

14th April, 2004

Mr. Robin Cooper,
Brondesbury Villas,
London

Dear Mr. Cooper,

I do apologise for the delay in replying to your letter dated 2nd March, 2004 which I received on 26th March, 2004.

Thank you for your letter and for kindly enclosing a stamped addressed envelope but, Mr. Cooper, I very much regret that I am unable to accede to your special (Point 4) request if you do decide to stay at Claridge's.

Yours sincerely,

Christopher Cowdray
MANAGING DIRECTOR

END OF CORRESPONDENCE

Robin Cooper
Brondesbury Villas
London

Mr Neil M Henderson-Begg
Secretary
The Hamper Industry Trade Association Ltd
North Ferriby
Hull
East Yorks.

23rd February 2004

Dear Mr –Begg,

I do hope this letter finds you in good steed, for I have had countenance of many wonderful things of your organization. May fortune smile 'pon you Sir.

I trust you do not mind the formality, only I have been brushing up on my etiquette of late. I can assure you that it does one no harm, au contraire, it does one NO harm!

Allow me to get to the point.

I understand that your marvellous organization represents the needs of those who are privileged enough to produce hampers for the general public. I use the word 'priviliged' as it is indeed a PRIVILIGE – nothing quite beats the receivership of said item (hamper).

Well, step forward a new producer of hampers – Robin Cooper (I). I have been designing both hampers - and the produce that sits within them – for a number of years now, and am at last ready to unveil my collection of hampers and hamperettes unto the nation.

But first, I will require some assistance from an expect (your good slef), and thus wonder whether I would be able to send you further details of my unique hamper/hamperettes, in order for you to advise me as to whether/whether not I am/am not going about/not going about things in the correct/incorrect 'manner'.

I thank you once again for your support and kindness, and enclose an SAE.

In yours, I remain,

Robin Cooper

HAMPER INDUSTRY TRADE ASSOCIATION LIMITED (By Guarantee)

25th February 2004

Mr Robin Cooper,
Brondesbury Villas,
London.

Dear Mr Cooper,

Thank you for your elegant letter which unfortunately was marred by two mistakes in paragraph No.6. "Expect" instead of (and here I am making what is probably a correct assumption) "expert" and "slef" instead of, probably "self" or possibly "serf" !

The Hamper Industry Trade Association's members are only those companies within the UK who market their hampers and associated Christmas orientated products through a network of 'housewife' agents who sell on a pre-payment basis to their friends, family and workmates, for which they receive commission once all payments and deliveries have been completed.

The contents of these hampers are for the most part basic foodstuffs, packed in decorated cardboard cartons. The hampers are not full of luxury foods packed in wicker baskets.

For your interest I enclose a copy of our "Be Sure" leaflet and our Code of Practice.

If you wish to send me a copy of your brochure or marketing material I will be happy to study it and give you my opinion.

Yours sincerely,

Neil Henderson-Begg
Secretary

Robin Cooper
Brondesbury Villas
London

Mr Neil M Henderson-Begg
Secretary
The Hamper Industry Trade Association Ltd
North Ferriby
Hull
East Yorks.

28th February 2004

Dear Mr –Begg,

Thank you greatly for your letter of 25th February. I was most touched.

I must begin by apologizing humbly for my two grammatical and syntaxical errors, which you deftly pointed out. Indeed, in paragraph 6 of my previous letter (copy enclosed), I did intend to use the word 'expert' but instead wrote (or typed) 'expect'. Similarly, the word 'self' became 'slef'. You clearly are a man with very good eyes! Hopefully this letter wil be error free.

I was delighted to learn that you would be interested in seeing some of my material, and I take pleasure in enclosing some hand-drawn sketches of my latest products.

I would welcome any feedback, and look forward to hearing from you.

In the meantime, many thanks again.

Best wishes,

Robin Cooper

Hampers/Hamperettes by Robin Cooper (Samples)

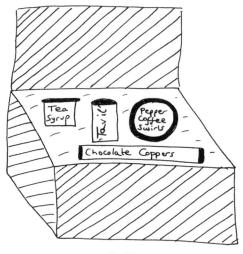

Tea Syrup

Tavic

Pepper Coffee Swirls

Chocolate Coppers

Hamper #61
'The Benson'

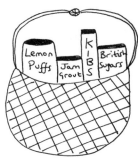

Lemon Puffs

Jam grout

KIBS

British Sugars

Hamperette #9
'The Rimini'

Lime Paste

Tibbys

Mutton Cubes

Hamperette #6
'Prismini'

END OF CORRESPONDENCE

64

Robin Cooper
Brondesbury Villas
London

David Beeton
Director General
The British Casino Association Ltd
Grosvenor Gardens
London

25th February 2004

Dear Mr Beeton,

I wonder if you can help.

I am planning to set up a gambling den at my premises within the next few months. Obviously I am aware of the tough competition, (what with the sheer number of famous betting dens around), and have thus been thinking long and hard as to my 'way in'.

And now I have it! I plan to open the very first branch of 'Lothium Kilvarno Hentmal', a gambling den that will corner one area of the market that has been, until now, completely untapped: the under 16's. That's because Lothium Kilvarno Hentmal will be the world's first betting den exclusively for children.

Can you tell me how I go about getting a licence, and, off the record, would you be prepared to invest some money (up to about £12,000) in Lothium Kilvano Hentmal? You could make a mint (mum's the word of course).

I look forward to hearing from you,

Best wishes,

Robin Cooper

Robin Cooper

BRITISH CASINO ASSOCIATION

Grosvenor Gardens London

26th February 2004

Mr Robin Cooper
Brondesbury Villas
London

Dear Mr Cooper

There are laws governing gambling in Great Britain and breach of these laws can lead to severe penalties, particularly in the case of children. Before you proceed I suggest you consult a lawyer versed in gambling law.

Yours sincerely

David Beeton
Director General

END OF CORRESPONDENCE

Robin Cooper
Brondesbury Villas
London

Cameron Clow
Secretary
The British Ladder Manufacturers Association
Broad Street
Glasgow

27th February 2004

Dear Mr Clow,

I have been working with ladders for over 12 years now, and can safely say I feel some kind of affinity with them. In other words, I really enjoy my work, and have never looked back (which is wise advice if you are up a ladder!!!!!!).

I have penned several poems about ladders and wonder if you would be so kind as to include them in your newsletter? Here is just a sample of one of them.

Up A Ladder by Robin Cooper

Step by step,
Climb the rungs,
Reaching up,
Towards the sun,
Above the street,
And the rooves,
See the horses,
But not their hooves.

For they are low down,
Beneath the beasts,
Clippety clop,
Through the streets,
Their tails swishing,
To and Fro,
I'm up a ladder,
Do say "hello"

Do you like it enough to publish it? I liked it enough to paint the words all over the one of my favourite aluminium ladders.

I look forward to hearing from you,

Best wishes

Robin Cooper

BRITISH LADDER MANUFACTURERS ASSOCIATION

Honorary Secretary, Mr Clow
C/o Broad Street
GLASGOW

30 March, 2004

CC/300304/01

Mr. Robin Cooper
Brondesbury Villas
London

Dear Mr. Cooper,

Thank you for taking time out of your busy schedule to pen your ladder poem. Unfortunately we do not have a newsletter that we could add your poem; however it was shown to the members present at our recent council meeting.

We would like to wish you every success in your writing and wish you continued enjoyment in using ladders and step ladders.

Sincerely,

Cameron Clow
Honorary Secretary

END OF CORRESPONDENCE

Robin Cooper
Brondesbury Villas
London

Mrs Valerie A Guggan
Members Coordinator
The Professional Darts Players Association
Federation House
Stoneleigh Park
Warks

27th February 2004

Dear Mrs Guggan,

One hundred and eighty!

Yes, I too am a fanatical darts player/fan, and have heard many fine things said of your organisation. Congratulation are thus due all around.

I am writing to you for some advice.

Over the past several years, I have been making changes to the traditional darts board, and have finally arrived at what, I believe, is a better board than the one that everyone uses (the traditional one).

Do you think you might be able to provide some of your professional darts players to 'road test' my board at some stage? I think they'd be most interested in my radical new design.

Would it be useful for me to send you a diagram of the board?

I look forward to hearing from you.

One hundred and eighty!

Best wishes,

Robin Cooper

PROFESSIONAL DART PLAYERS ASSOCIATION

Cooper0304/TDA/vad

22 March 2004

Mr Robin Cooper
Brondesbury Villas
London

Dear Mr Cooper

Thank you for your letter regarding your new design darts board, which I will bring to the attention of the Board of the Professional Darts Players Association at their next meeting, after which I will write to you again.

I will also pass your letter on to a manufacturer who is a member of our Federation and who might be interested in communicating with you.

Regards.

Yours sincerely

V A DUGGAN
Association Manager

Federation House, Stoneleigh Park, Warwickshire

Cooper0304/Test/Board/vad

25 March 2004

Mr Robin Cooper
Brondesbury Villas
London

Dear Mr Cooper

Your letter regarding your new design darts board was brought to the attention of the Board of the Professional Darts Players Association at their meeting on Tuesday, 23 March 2004.

The Board members have said that they would be quite happy to 'road test' your board. If you could let me have six dart boards I will pass them on to the Board members, who will then report back to you with their comments.

Regards.

Yours sincerely

V A DUGGAN
Association Manager

Federation House, Stoneleigh Park, Warwickshire

Robin Cooper
Brondesbury Villas
London

Mrs Valerie A Duggan
Members Coordinator
The Professional Darts Players Association
Federation House
Stoneleigh Park
Warks

2nd April 2004

Dear Mrs Duggan,

Many thanks for your letter of 25th March. May I first begin by apologising deeply for addressing you as Mrs 'Guggan' in my previous letter. I do not know quite how this happened, as I am usually extremely thorough regarding syntax and soforth. I trust you were not too hurt.

Privy thee.

You kindly asked me to send you six of my new radically-altered dart boards, for which I was most touched. I do hope you understand that I am unable to do this, as I fear they may get lost in the post. However, if your members would like to see (and play) (with) one of my dart boards, I have one hanging at the 'Grand Messiter' pub in Stiltsbury. The owner - a Mr K.C.W Turrant - was so impressed with my design, that he hastily consigned his dart board to the dustbin – not of history, but of literally.

If this is not possible, I would be happy to send you the designs to my board.

I look forward to hearing from you, and once again, many apologies for the incorrect spelling of your surname. As punishment, I will deliberately misspell my name at the bottom of the page.

One hundred and eighty!

Best wishes,

Robin Looper

 **PROFESSIONAL DART PLAYERS ASSOCIATION**

Cooper0404/Test/Board/vad

7 April 2004

Mr Robin Cooper
Brondesbury Villas
London

Dear Mr Cooper

Thank you for your reply of 2 April 2004 to my letter of 25 March regarding the Board members testing your revolutionary dart board.

I will pass on the information about the location of your board in Stiltsbury to the Board members. The members can then decide if they wish to take up the opportunity of 'playing' the board should they be in the area.

In the meantime, if you would like to send me a copy of the design of your dart board, I will bring it to the attention of the Board at their next meeting, after which I will report back to you their comments.

Yours sincerely

V A DUGGAN
Association Manager

Federation House, Stoneleigh Park, Warwickshire

Robin Cooper
Brondesbury Villas
London

Mrs Valerie A Duggan
Members Coordinator
The Professional Darts Players Association
Federation House
Stoneleigh Park
Warks

10th April 2004

Dear Mrs Duggan,

Many thanks for your wonderful letter of 7th April, in reply to mine of 2nd April, in reply to yours of 25th March in reply to mine of 27th February. I also trust you had a lovely Easter.

I herewin take great pleasure in enclosing a sketch of my revolutionary dart board - an actual, physical copy of which is currently hanging, as I mentioned previously, in the 'Grand Messiter' pub in Stiltsbury.

You will notice that I have made several, radical changes to the board: firstly, I have dispensed with the traditional 'round' shape, and opted for a rectangular board. Numbered areas are triangular along the flanks of the board, and squaral through the middle.

The clear markings (i.e. numberings and letterings), used throughout, makes the board both easy to play and hopefully, visually appealing. The board is currently set in yellow and brown, with blue for the 'Bullseye' section.

I wonder what your members think of it. Would you be prepared to financially back the board? I am looking for a figure of around £22,000 to really get this board on the market.

I look forward to hearing from you.

Best wishes,

Robin Cooper

Robin Cooper's New Dart Board

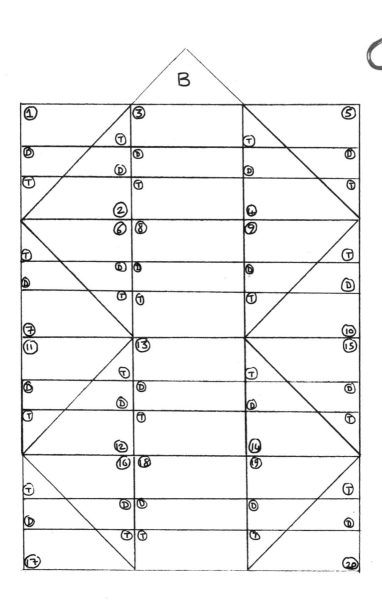

Key: Ⓓ = Double
Ⓣ = Treble
Ⓑ = Bullseye!

END OF CORRESPONDENCE

75

Robin Cooper
Brondesbury Villas
London

Michael Hudson
Honorary Secretary
The British Unidentified Flying Objects Research Association
High Street
Wingham
Kent

27th February 2004

Dear Mr Hudson,

Am I glad to have found (out about) your organisation!

My wife and I believe each other to have both witnessed what we would describe as a UFO (Unidentified Flying Object). Two days after the event, we are still shaking from shock.

It all happened two days ago when I was taking my wife to hospital for a routine check-up on her ankle. Her ankle has been poorly for some time now, and requires regular medical attention, but that is beside the point.

As we drove towards the hospital gates, we suddenly noticed a rotating 'disc' shaped object in the sky, from which emanated lots of multi-coloured lights. Within moments our car started to shake whilst being bathed in a powerful red and blue light. During this my wife and I both heard a shrill voice inside our heads repeating the phrase "Take not in, take not out. Use the 95th key".

Then all went silent, and the car stopped shaking. My wife and I looked out of the window but the 'disc' was gone. When I inspected my car, I found its battery to be leaking, and a symbol shaped like an owl had been burnt into the bonnet.

Do you have any idea what this 'disc' was? Has anyone else reported it? What is the significance of the owl? What does the phrase "Take not in, take not out. Use the 95th key" mean?

I have some sketches of the 'disc' and the owl markings – would you care to see them?

I look forward to your reply.

Best wishes,

Robin Cooper

British UFO Research Association

Judith Jaafar
Castlebar Road
Ealing
London W5

Mr. Robin Cooper
Brondesbury Villas
London

25/3/04

Dear Mr. Cooper,

Thank you for contacting BUFORA about your recent anomalous event. Firstly, may I apologise for this rather late reply – we have recently lost our secretary and it has taken some time for all communications to be forwarded to me, as I have temporarily taken over admin duties.

Your account sounds very interesting, and we would be pleased if you could fill out the enclosed report form in as much detail as possible. It would be useful if you would include copies of your sketches also. Please return the form to me at the Ealing address.

After careful evaluation of the material you send, it may be appropriate for myself or a colleague to meet up with you and discuss the case, if you are willing.

Looking forward to receiving your reply.

Yours sincerely,

Judy Jaafar
BUFORA Chairman

Robin Cooper
Brondesbury Villas
London

Judy Jaafar
BUFORA Chairman
The British Unidentified Flying Objects Research Association
High Street
Wingham
Kent CT3 1BJ

9th April 2004

Dear Ms Jaafar,

Many thanks for your letter of 25th March. I was saddened to hear that you lost your secretary recently. I am sorry.

As promised, here is a sketch of the 'disc' my wife and I saw and also the mysterious 'owl' markings on my bonnet.

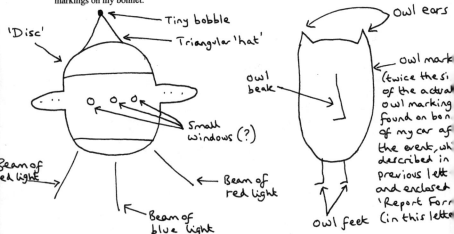

I also take pleasure in enclosing a completed 'report form', which I trust is of use.

I look forward to hearing from you.

Best wishes,

Robin Cooper

Robin Cooper

QUESTIONNAIRE

Full Name

Mr Robin Cooper

Address

Brondesbury Villas

London

Date of Birth

Too personal !!

Telephone Number

Do not have one

Recent Occupation

Self-employed

**Professional, technical
or academic qualifications**

I'd rather not list these, for personal reasons.

Special Interests/Hobbies

Too many to mention here!!

WRITTEN ACCOUNT   Please write an account of what happened to you

On the 25th February 2004, I was taking my wife to hospital (by car), because she has a recurring bad ankle problem. When we neared the hospital gates, we saw a rotating 'disc' object in the heavens (sky). Lights of many colours came from it (the disc). Our car shook violently and was covered in a blue + red light (but not purple as the colours were <u>not</u> mixed together). My wife and I both heard a horrible, piercing voice inside our heads repeating the phrase, "Take not in, take not out. Use the 95th key!"

Then the car stopped shaking and the 'disc' disappeared. My car battery was left leaking, and a symbol much like an <u>owl</u> had appeared to have been burnt into the bonnet.

It was all <u>very</u>, <u>very</u>, <u>VERY</u> strange.

OBJECT CHARACTERISTICS
Please use this space to sketch what you saw

①

'Disc' seen in sky by my
wife and I in our car.

②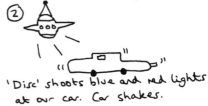

'Disc' shoots blue and red lights
at our car. Car shakes.

③

Battery

With 'Disc' gone, car is inspected
(by me). Battery has leaked.

④

Symbol of <u>owl</u> burnt into car bonne⟶

Number of Objects seen

1

Colour(s) of Object(s) seen

Silver/pink

Brightness of object(s) seen

Compared to the brightness of full moon

slightly less bright

Sound of object(s) seen

silent

Smell of object(s) seen

slight smell of violets

THE PHYSICAL CHARACTERISTICS OF THE OBSERVATION

1. Date and time of observation

25th February 2004, at 7:30pm

2. Duration of observation

Duration more than......30......mins/(secs)

But less than......2......(mins)/secs

3. Regarding questions 1 and 2. How did you gauge the time duration?

My wife and I both guessed.

4. Where were you at the time of the incident?
including nearest street, town or village

In our car.

5. What first brought your attention to the incident?

The 'disc' was very bright, and just caught our (my wife and my) attention.

6. How did the object(s) disappear from view?

Vanished.

7. Comparing the size of the object(s) you saw to that of the full moon, was it:-

(Smaller   Bigger   The same size   Larger
Give details)   circle if appropriate give details

8. Was the object(s) photographed, filmed or video recorded? if yes, give details

Sadly no. It was neither photographed, filmed, or video recorded. I wish we had done any one of the above options.

9. Were there any other witnesses to the object(s) you saw?
if yes, give names, addresses and telephone numbers where possible

No.

10. Did you, or the surrounding environment, suffer any physical effects which you consider to be attributable to the object(s) seen?

Very shaken up. My wife's bad ankle worsened.

11. Were you aware of the passage of time around the time of the observation?
if no, describe

No. It was like being in a 'time sack'.

12. If you have had any other unusual experience in your life describe them.

I once met the Queen when I least expected it.
Other than that, not really.

13. Other than the event you have reported, did anything else odd or out of place occur around the time of the observation?
if yes, describe

No, although we noticed an abundance of crows flying above our car immediately after. About a thousand.

Witness' Signature

R. Lin Cooper

Date

8/4/04

Robin Cooper
Brondesbury Villas
London

Judy Jaafar
BUFORA Chairman
The British Unidentified Flying Objects Association
High Street
Wingham
Kent

9th May 2004

Dear Ms Jaafar,

Verily do I hope that you are well.

I wonder if you can help: I wrote to you back in April, enclosing a completed 'report form', following my incident with the strange disc I saw along with my wife.

I trust you have been busy of late, as I am yet to receive a reply. However, my wife and I are very keen to hear your thoughts on our shared incident.

I (we) look forward to hearing from you.

Best wishes,

Robin Cooper

**The Association for the Scientific
Study of Anomalous Phenomena**

George Thomas Gregg MSc, MA, CertEd
National Investigations Coordinator
Specialist Knowledge Coordinator: Altered States

20th May, 2004

Dear Mr Cooper,

Please accept my apologies for the delay in responding to your letter regarding

a clearly distressing and frightening experience. The features of your report do

match other UFO type reports unfortunately I was unable to fathom the meaning

of 'Take not in, take not out. Use the 95th Key'. However Steve Poole of UFO Research

Midlands would like to follow up the case. I'm enclosing a report form. If you could

complete it (with your diagrams) and post it on to him he will take things from there.

- **Address: UFO Research Midlands**
  PO Box 1052
  Brierley Hill
  West Midlands
  DY5 3ZF

Do not hesitate to contact me if I can be of any further help
Yours truly,

George Gregg NIC (ASSAP)
National Investigations Coordinator

20/5/04.

84

Robin Cooper
Brondesbury Villas
London

Steve Poole
UFO Research Midlands
PO Box 1052
Brierley Hill
West Midlands

25th May 2004

Dear Steve,

You do not know me (sadly), but you will see from the enclosed correspondence that George Gregg NIC invited me to write to you.

Thus, I am hereby doing so.

As requested by George, I am enclosing a further report form for your convenience.

Can you help? My wife and I are still at a loss as to what the disc was, what the owl means and what the phrase, "Take not in, take not out. Use the 95th key" signifies?

I look forward to hearing from you.

Best wishes,

Robin Cooper

UFORM - Sightings Report Form
UFORM. P.O. Box 1052, Brierley Hill, West Midlands, DY5 3ZF

Date: 25th Feb 2004	Time: 7:30 pm
Duration: Probably 1 minute	Probably until 7:31 (is this correct?)
Description of Object/Entity.	
Number 1 object/entity	
Size	Quite large
Shape	Disc with a sort of 'hat' on top
Colours	Silver/pink
Brightness	Quite bright
Sound	Silent
Smell	Violets
Exact Position Of Observer. Geographical Location Indoors/Outdoors Stationary/Moving	We were in our car (my wife + I) at Barnet Hospital due to my wife's bad ankle. The car was outdoors. We had stopped in the car.
How Object Was Observed: Naked Eye Binoculars/Telescope Still Camera Video Camera	We observed the object/entity with naked eyes, although to this day I wish I had packed our sets of binoculars and/or telescope.
Angle Of Sight:	
Distance: (Refer to landmarks)	Don't understand this. Sorry!
Movement Of Object:	In sky, so hard to say. 200 metres? Rotating disc object. It moved a little bit - from left to right and then at the end just disappeared like magic
Meteorological Conditions:	Cold.
Nearby Objects or Buildings:	Hospital
To Whom Reported:	Calvin Hemley
Contact First Name Only* and Phone No:	Calvin. He does not own phones

British UFO Research Association

Rothbury Terrace
Heaton
Newcastle Upon tyne

Date: 16th September 2004

Dear Robin

Many thanks for your letter of 9th May 2004 and I would like to extend my apologies for the delay in responding. Unfortunately, we have had a change of central office at BUFORA and this has generated many delays in correspondence being forwarded to the relevant people.

Many thanks for your completed questionnaire, which I also have received.

As you do not have a telephone, I think the best way forward here would be if I forwarded your completed questionnaire to Judy Jaafar, who lives in Ealing, West London. I will ask that she writes to you and then you could telephone her to set up an appointment for her to come and talk with you and your wife and obtain more information on this sighting.

Thank you for contacting BUFORA and please feel free to contact me if you have any questions.

Yours sincerely

Gloria Heather Dixon

Gloria Heather Dixon
Director of Investigations

END OF CORRESPONDENCE

Robin Cooper
Brondesbury Villas
London

Janice Houghton-Wallace
Honorary Secretary & Treasurer
Turkey Club UK
Graycoats
Great Eversden
Cambridge

15th March 2004

Dear Janice,

Aren't turkeys such marvellous creatures? I had one once and it was absolutely lovely. We named him (or was it her?!) 'Telvosky', although why we did so (the naming of) we never seem to remember!

That aside, I am writing to ask you to ask for some advice.

I would very much like to become a judge at a professional turkey show. I have seen the dog ones, but they look a little too hard for an amateur like me. Turkeys, I assume, are easier to judge because they are smaller creatures, hence less time needed to check for nits etc.

Although I am not properly experienced, I have a keen eye, a semi-professional demeanour and a love of turkeys.

I really do LOVE turkeys. Look:

Do you think I would fit the 'bill' (please excuse the pun!).

I look forward to hearing from you, and thank you in advance for your time.

Robin Cooper

NO RESPONSE

87

Robin Cooper
Brondesbury Villas
London

Ralph Moore-Morris
Secretary
The Victorian Military Society
Franks Road
Guildford
Surrey

23rd March 2004

Dear Mr –Morris,

I have heard innumerable wonderful things about your organization, and thus I wonder if you can help.

I have always been fascinated with military history, in particular the Victorian era. Charles Penningworth, Lord Hebworth, Marie de Halles, are just some of the names that I have enjoyed from that period, the period of Victoriana.

With this in mind, for the last six months I have been renovating my attic so that it resembles a Victorian officer's drawing room from the 1890's. Inside you will find all that you would expect from such a room; a Chippendale chest of drawers, a Victorian tiara (mounted atop a stuffed ox!) and a set of de Montfort cluffys (originals).

Now that the room is complete, I intend to live inside it as a fully-fledged Victorian officer for a period of six months. Indeed I will eat, sleep and bathe in the one room (my wife and children will make their own living arrangements away from the house).

Here's where you come in…

In order to make this whole thing seem real, I require one period manservant, one period cook, and one period doctor, all of whom will spend the six months living with me in the one room. Their role will be to stay in character at all times, acting out various domestic scenarios, which I have already written. What I'd like to know is whether you can provide me with these people from your organisation? In exchange I can offer each of them a decent wage, albeit at 1890's rates.

I think you will agree that this is a social experiment of the highest order. Are you in?

I look forward to your response and trust that you will be able to assist.

With very best Victorian wishes,

Robin Cooper

Robin Cooper's Attic / Gentleman's Drawing Room from the 1890's

emerald of St. Kitts

hook in wall

Victorian tiara

rope

ox (stuffed)

Cupboard containing
Victorian supplies
(molasses, quinine,
quills etc.) *

grandfather clock

oversized vase

pendulum

ornate box containing
set of de Montfort
Cluffys (originals)

pendulum's
weight

base of clock

coal

fireplace
(sadly in disuse)

Chippendale set of drawers

plate of toffees

decorative bowl
(for washing + drinking)

R jug

My bed
(eiderdown)

Doctor's bed
(feathers)

cotton
sheets

flannellette pillow

stethoscope

down + silk pillows

Cook's bed
(also feathers)

woollen sheets

fine linen
sheets

sack cloth pillow

cooking
pan

Maidservant's bed
atop straw mattress

rough hemp sheets

my nightcap

charity box

hessian pillow

* Also doubles as Water closet

89

Mr R Cooper
Brondesbury Villas
LONDON

14 April 2004

Dear Mr Cooper

Many thanks for your letter of 23rd March addressed to our Secretary, which has been passed to me. I apologise for the delay in replying caused by the forwarding and my absence from home.

We are most appreciative of your kind comments regarding the Victorian Military Society and your project is certainly original and will no doubt prove to be a most interesting experiment. Unfortunately we are unable to assist with your request for 'staff' as we have nobody within our membership who would be interested.

Thank you again for contacting us and I wish you every success with the project.

Yours Sincerely

C.B.L. KEMPTON [CHAIRMAN, VICTORIAN MILITARY SOCIETY]
SELBOURNE ROAD. GILLINGHAM. KENT.

END OF CORRESPONDENCE

Robin Cooper
Brondesbury Villas
London

Customer Services
Safeway Head Office
Millington Road
Hayes
Middlesex UB3 4AY

8th April 2004

Dear Sir or Madam,

I wonder if you can help.

Are Safeway Supermarkets interested in helping me raise money for charity? I do hope so…

I am planning to raise over £1000 by embarking on a nationwide 'Sponsored Hair-Drying'. The idea is quite simple really: I turn up at one of your many stores (I believe you have at least 15 – do correct me if I'm wrong), and clear a small space in one of the aisles. My wife then proceeds to wet my hair thoroughly using water from one of Safeway's own brand of bottled water. I then wash my hair using a Safeway brand shampoo, rinse off with the Safeway brand of bottled water, wash with a Safeway conditioner, before rinsing again with the Safeway brand of bottled water. Now for the drying: after patting down with a Safeway towel, my wife plugs in a Safeway's own hair-dryer (either to the mains or to a generator that WE CAN SUPPLY), and dries my hair until it is TOTALLY and UTTERLY dry. I repeat this process 50 times each day.

Along the way customers (and staff if pressed) donate money - either for the amount of times I dry my hair, or for some other factor (for example, money may be bid against the wetness of my hair and offset against dryness, all on a sliding percentage scale).

That, in short, is it. My aim is to bring my 'Sponsored Hair-Drying' to every Safeway Supermarket up and down the land. I have calculated that with only 15 stores, that's about 3 weeks hair drying.

I am ready to start right away, so would be grateful if you could confirm what date I should begin, and indeed what store I need to report to. Also, are you happy for me to discuss this with the press in the meantime?

I look forward to hearing from you.

Best wishes,

Robin Cooper

Our ref: 545452a

23 April 2004

Mr R Cooper
Brondesbury Villas
London

Safeway Stores plc
Customer Services
Beddow Way
Aylesford
Nr Maidstone
Kent
ME20 7AT

Dear Mr Cooper

Thank you for your letter of 8th April 2004 seeking support for your charity.

This opportunity has been given full consideration by our senior management but I regret that because of previous commitments and budget constraints we are unable to assist on this occasion.

I hope you will understand that we receive many requests for all sorts of help and it is just not possible for us to respond to each one in the way we would wish.

I wish you every success in gaining the support you are seeking; I am sorry we cannot assist, but I should like to thank you for the interest you have shown in approaching us.

Yours sincerely

Emma Gowers
Customer Services Department

END OF CORRESPONDENCE

**Robin Cooper
Brondesbury Villas
London**

M Adams
Administrator
The Good Gardeners Association
Lisle Place
Wotton-under-Edge
Glos.

10th May 2004

Dear Mr Adams,

From one green-fingered man to another, I salute you. Hark 'o Gardener of Grandeur!

I too am a keen organic gardener, and have come to hear many fine things said of your organisation. One person (Thomas Van Guuten) said "Traabs men haus-gehan jivein!" And that was just in his language!

I do hope you enjoyed my joke, but you are no doubt a busy man, so I will get to the point.

I have recently acquired 14 tons of organic clay soil. I am planning to fashion the soil into a 'living statue' depicting an enormous pair of plyers battling with an ashtray full of carrots. The aim being to symbolise man (the plyers) fighting corporate greed (ashtray) vis-à-vis poor gardening practices (carrots).

I plan to place this 'living monument' in London's Piccadilly Circus (I will probably do it at night so less people see me).

Will you support my campaign? All I require is a nod, and I am ready to go!

I look forward to hearing from you.

With green-fingered best wishes,

[signature]

Robin Cooper

Being honest I don't quite understand the symbolism but I wish you well in your endeavours

Mr. M. C. Adams
17/5/04.

END OF CORRESPONDENCE

93

Robin Cooper
Brondesbury Villas
London

David and Judith Robinson
Honorary Treasurers
Association for Marriage Enrichment
Between Streets
Cobham
Surrey

10th May 2004

Dear Both David and Judith,

From what I have been told, your organisation is devoted to the fine work of helping marriages (those glorious coming togethers of men and wives), to function properly, decently and with good faith throughout.

Congratulations are thus in order to you both.

CONGRATULATIONS!

That said, I myself am a devoted husband and have spent most of my married life developing ideas as to the enrichment of said marriage. I now have a number of fascinating tips that you might like to hear (of).

May I send you these tips?

I look forward to hearing from you both – but there's no need to write two separate letters…one will suffice!!!!

With very best wishes,

Robin Cooper

Association for Marriage Enrichment
Focus on Couples

Please reply to: David and Judith Robinson
Between Streets, Cobham,
SURREY

21 May 2004

Robin Cooper
Brondesbury Villas
London

Dear Robin

Thank you very much for your letter of encouragement.

We thought that in view of your commitment to marriage, you and your wife might perhaps like to come on one of our AME events, so that we can all share our experience of what makes a good marriage. Do have a look at our Website, as shown at the head of this letter, for a list of forthcoming events. Alternatively we would be happy just to receive your list of tips: we are always ready to discover something new!

Just to bring you up to date, Judith and I are no longer Treasurers, although we still both serve on the AME Executive committee.

With our very best wishes

David & Judith Robinson
AME

Robin Cooper
Brondesbury Villas
London

David and Judith Robinson
Servants of the AME Executive Committee
Association for Marriage Enrichment
Between Streets
Cobham
Surrey

27th May 2004

Dear Both David and Judith,

Thank you whole wheartedly for your charming letter of 21st May in reply to my letter (of encouragement) of 10th May previous.

I should indeed be honoured to send you my list of Tips on Marriage Enrichment, and thus, enclose them below. As you will see, they come in the form of an A-Z (list):

Always say "Good morning" in the morning.
Be careful to be presentable, even during slumber.
Cast thy mind back to whence thee were young. We all make mistakes!
Dedication. Dedicarus. Decorum.
End all arguments with a gentle sigh and a flourish of the hat.
Find a golden penny in every pound.
Go for a walk together thrice daily.
Helvetian glimpses give more a scurry sailor!
Indecision is the route to infidelity.
Join hands on your thrice-daily walk.
Knights in shining armour always find their fayre maiden.
Let the light in, whence it becomes dark.
Maidens fayre shall their knights in shining armour find.
Nothing shall get in thy way – save love.
Open thine eyes to thy partner's (eyes).
Procure harmony whence there is lack of cordiality.
Quiet! Quiet! Quiet! Thy love may be sleeping!
Rinse all dishes thoroughly when washing.
Stand upright in the presence of thy elders.
Tomorrow is another day, but today is only tomorrow, yesterday.
Unless called for, do not bang on pots and pans.
Vexation is the devil's hand-cart. Snip his wheels and the devil doth run to ruin.
While the day away, while the day whiles the away, away!
X – (nothing for X unfortunately).
Yuletide tidings – all year around!
Zealous love, jealous love. Jealous love, zealous love.

I do hope you like it. Will you publish it?

I did try to find your 'Website' but couldn't as I do not have access to the 'intanet'. Apologies in abundance.

I look forward to hearing from you.

With best wishes,

Robin Cooper

Robin Cooper

David and Judith Robinson
Between Streets, Cobham,
SURREY

3 June 2004

Robin Cooper
Brondesbury Villas
London

Dear Robin

Thank you very much for your list of maxims. You have obviously given the question of good marriage a lot of thought.

You haven't indicated whether you are married yourself, but if you are, we are sure that you would find one of our weekend training events valuable. Please have a look at the enclosed leaflet, which gives some idea as to what happens on our weekends and what they are about. There are two 6-week evening courses planned in the London area for September/October and a weekend course in November. The leaflet shows how to obtain further details.

With our very best wishes

David + Judith

David & Judith Robinson
AME

Robin Cooper
Brondesbury Villas
London

David and Judith Robinson
Servants of the AME Executive Committee
Association for Marriage Enrichment
Between Streets
Cobham
Surrey

12th June 2004

Dear Both David and Judith,

I was so touched to receive your GLORIOUS letter of the 3rd June. I was also GLORIFIED when I read the contents of it.

As my photocopier is on the blink at the moment (boar gnawed through cable at weekend), I shall retype your letter, just in case you did not keep a copy for yourselves.

"Thank you very much for your (my) list of maxims. You (I) have obviously given the question of good marriage a lot of thought.

You (I) haven't indicated whether you (I) are (am) married yourself (myself), but if you (I) are (am), we (you) are sure that you (I) would find one of our (your) weekend training events valuable. Please have a look at the enclosed leaflet, which gives some ideas as to what happens on our weekends and what they are about. There are two 6-week evening courses planned in the London area for September/October and a weekend course in November. The leaflet shows how to obtain details.

With our (your) very best wishes,

David & Judith Robinson, AME"

I trust this refreshes your memory. In answer to the above, I am indeed married - a fact I did point out in my first letter. Indeed, I said (and I quote), "I (I) myself am a devoted husband". Hopefully this will have answered your question.

My wife and I enjoyed your GLORIOUS leaflet, and would very much like to attend one of your events. However, we would like to know: is my wife and I allowed to bring along our own waste paper basket with us during our stay?

I look forward to hearing from you before booking up with you.

Best wishes,

Robin Cooper

Robin Cooper
Brondesbury Villas
London

David and Judith Robinson
Servants of the AME Executive Committee
Association for Marriage Enrichment
Between Streets
Cobham
Surrey

18th June 2004

Dear Both David and Judith,

Thank you heartily for sending me your leaflet entitled 'Focus On Couples'. It was packed with GLORIOUS and USEFUL information.

However, I think you may have forgotten to enclose your reply letter, as it was missing from the envelope. But don't fret the both of you, for even I have done this before…

Several years ago, I received a letter from a cousin of mine (I forget his name), who lived in Cherbourg, La France. In it, he (oh yes, his name was Pierre-Le-Prince), asked me if I should like to receive 4 bottles of '*Verrimantilier*' – a type of wine brewed using cherry stones instead of grapes.

I wrote back to him in the affirmative, but foolishly forgot to enclose the letter. A few months later, I received another letter from Pierre-Le-Prince saying that, as I hadn't replied (and merely sent an empty '*envelope*' (which is the same word in French by the way)), he had given the wine to someone else.

Thus we live and learn….

Anyway, I am sure you have your reply letter somewhere! If you recall, I wanted to book one of your weekends but was eager to know, and I quote:

"…is my wife and I allowed to bring along our own waste paper basket with us during our stay?"

I look forward to hearing from you and apologise for any inconvenience caused.

Yours respectfully,

Robin Cooper

Association for Marriage Enrichment
Focus on Couples

Please reply to: David and Judith Robinson
Between Streets, Cobham,
SURREY

21st June 2004

Robin Cooper
Brondesbury Villas
London

Dear Robin

We hadn't enclosed a letter because we didn't feel one was necessary. The leaflet contained all the information you need to find out about our events and to make a booking. This should be done via our Administrator Ali Foyle, not through ourselves.

You asked about bringing your own waste-paper basket. Our event organisers usually make sure that participants have access to all the equipment and materials they need. But if you feel you need to bring something special of your own, that's fine.

With our very best wishes

David & Judith

David & Judith Robinson
AME

Robin Cooper
Brondesbury Villas
London

Dr D Giachardi
Secretary General
The Royal Society of Chemistry
Burlington House
Piccadilly
London

1st July 2004

Dear Doctor D,

'Tis a pleasure to gain your acquaintance, and I wonder if you can help.

I have a keen interest in chemistry, and in particular, the field of filtration.

I have been filtering various items for nearing a decade now (10 years). I do this from home, as my shed - when it is not being used by my boar - is my very own filtration laboratory.

I wonder, however, if you could advise me as to where I can find the following pieces of (filtration) equipment:

1) Filtration 'heads' – I need about 40 of these, in conjunction with a new project involving the filtration of ant seed.
2) Filter paper markers – I am looking for round ones if possible as the hexagonal markers keep slipping off.
3) Paper vessel holders/stirrups. I cannot seem to find these anywhere.
4) Finally – Ash devellium free-standing filter lights. I need two.

I thank you for your help in advance, and please except my apologies for any inconvenience caused.

I am enclosing a SAE and look forward to hearing from you.

With very best (unfiltered) wishes!

Robin Cooper

Dr. D.J. Giachardi MA DPhil CChem FRSC
Secretary General and Chief Executive

Mr. R. Cooper,
Brondesbury Villas
London

Burlington House
Piccadilly
London
United Kingdom

DJG/pc
21st July 2004

Dear Mr. Cooper,

With reference to your letter of enquiry dated 1st July 2004, I list below details of two suppliers who should be able to assist you in your quest for filtration equipment.

Fisher Scientific Ltd.
Bishop Meadow Road
Loughborough
Leicestershire

Sigma-Aldrich Company Ltd.
The Old Brickyard
New Road
Gillingham
Dorset

Yours sincerely,

D. J. Giachardi

David Giachardi

Robin Cooper
Brondesbury Villas
London

Sigma-Aldrich Company Ltd
The Old Brickyard
New Road
Gillingham
Dorset

31st July 2004

Dear Sir/Madam,

Please allow your good self to be referred back to the (enclosed) corrrespondi.

Doctor D, of the Royal Society of Chemistry, was kind enough to pass on your details, as I am currently looking for the following filtration equipment:

10) Filtration 'heads' – I NOW need 65 of these, in conjunction with a new project involving the filtration of ant seed.
11) Filter paper markers – I am looking for round ones if possible as the hexagonal markers keep slipping off.
12) Paper vessel holders/stirrups. I cannot seem to find these anywhere.
13) Ash devellium free-standing filter lights. I NOW need four.
14) Semi-permeable papers - for onion filtrate solution work.
15) Dust-free particle developers (plus tripod) – (not the 'Linthorpe' models though).
16) Anti-listing papers, with separate grips.
17) Divisisional vessel amulets (if possible, in sets of two)
18) FINALLY – 20 filter paper recorders.

Many thanks for your time.

Best wishes,

Robin Cooper

PS – You will note that the list is longer than the one I sent to Doctor D. Alas, that is but for the passing of time.

SIGMA-ALDRICH

SIGMA-ALDRICH COMPANY LTD
The Old Brickyard, New Road
Gillingham, Dorset

Robin Cooper
Brondesbury Villas
London

Robin,

Thank you for contacting us regarding your filtration requirements. Unfortunately, our licence does not allow us to supply materials to private individuals or to residential addresses. Thus, while we do have most of the equipment you require. By law, we will be unable to supply these to you.

Regards

TomSanAgustin

Tom San Agustin
European Technical Services
Sigma Aldrich

END OF CORRESPONDENCE

FS29169

We are Committed to the Success of our Customers, Employees and Shareholders through Leadership in Life Science, High Technology and Service

David Gordon
Secretary
The Royal Academy of Arts
Burlington House
Piccadilly
London W1J 0BD

2nd July 2004

Dear Mr Gordon,

I am, no doubt like your good self, a lover of art, and the arts – although not always of the artists!!

As you can see, there are exactly 100 '!''s above. Each '!' representing a year in art over the past century.

I'll get to the point.

Will you allow me to perform a one-man show in your gallery, some time over the next month or so?

Basically, this would involve me spray painting the word 'Themt' all over the ceiling. While this is going on, one thousand pieces of A4 paper are counted, one thousand times, by one thousand husbands. Their thousand wives must wait outside until this is finished.

At the end, we all run amok in the gallery, smashing exhibits and windows.

Do you like it enough to sponsor the show?

I do hope so.

I look forward to hearing from you.

Best wishes,

Robin Cooper

NO RESPONSE

105

Robin Cooper
Brondesbury Villas
London

Frank Broomhead
Honorary Secretary
The Private Libraries Association
Kenton
Harrow
Middlesex

2nd July 2004

Dear Mr Broomhead,

I am almost ready to open my own private library, which I intend to run from an old dilapidated barge that I have recently had reconditioned.

The barge has been cut down to a 'manageable' length (approx 80 ft), and can be towed by a couple of lorries using reinforced steel wire, with both vehicles sharing a large central stabilising rod. I plan to unveil the library barge in a couple of months (probably outside Chichester Cathedral for maximum impact).

With the launch date rapidly approaching, I wonder if you can help.

Would you be kind enough to lend me a few thousand of your books, as we only have about 40 at the moment. The usual stuff should do – fiction, non-fiction, romance, fencing annuals etc.

In return I am prepared to give you free (private) library membership.

I look forward to hearing from you and thank you in advance.

Best wishes,

R. Li Co

Robin Cooper

PRIVATE LIBRARIES ASSOCIATION

Honorary Vice-President: Frank Broomhead
Kenton, Harrow, Middlesex

7 July 2004

Robin Cooper, Esq.,
Brondesbury Villas,
London

Dear Mr Cooper,

I was interested to receive your letter of 2nd July 2004 and to learn of your proposal to open your private library in an old barge. I am not certain whether your letter was addressed to me personally, or in my capacity as Honorary Secretary of the Private Libraries Association, an office which I have now resigned but subsequently have been appointed Honorary Vice-President of that body..

Answering your letter both personally, and also in part on behalf of the Association, much as I must praise your decision to open your private library I fear that I do not consider any of my books suitable for the purpose you suggest, and in any case I would not wish to expose them to the obvious risks that your plan would indicate. I have discussed your proposal with one or two members of the PLA and without any prompting from me their reaction was identical to mine.

I am sorry to give such a negative response to your initiative, nevertheless, in spite of my views, I hope that I shall hear of the success of your venture.

Yours sincerely,

Frank Broomhead

END OF CORRESPONDENCE

Robin Cooper
Brondesbury Villas
London

Nigel Harding
Honorary Secretary
The International Guild of Knot Tyers
Uckfield
East Sussex

2nd July 2004

Dear Mr Harding,

I was given your organisation's name from a trusted friend, whose name I sadly forget. Nevertheless, he (or was it she?!), spoke extremely highly of your guild.

So, congratulations are in order.

CONGRATULATIONS!!!!!!

Never mind all that! The reason I am writing, is that I have always been fascinated with knots and knot tying, and, of late, have set about devising new knots and new methods of tying (and untying) them.

Having just returned from a mini speaking tour of Belgium, I wonder if you would be interested in seeing some diagrams of my new knots.

Well, would you?

I look forward to hearing from you.

Best wishes, and keep up the good work.

Robin Cooper

Robin Cooper

THE INTERNATIONAL GUILD OF KNOT TYERS
Hon. Secretary: Nigel Harding, Uckfield, East Sussex

Dear Robin,
Thanks for your letter, – my apologies for the delay in replying, but I have been away from my desk for some time, and I am only just catching up.
Yes – I would be interested in seeing your diagrams and your methods – Best wishes
N.H.

With Compliments

108

Robin Cooper
Brondesbury Villas
London

Nigel Harding
Honorary Secretary
The International Guild of Knot Tyers
Uckfield
East Sussex

4th October 2004

Dear Mr Harding,

Many thanks for your letter written 'pon a compliment slip. I was heartened to receive it, regardless of the lapsing of time.

I too must apologise for my late reply, for I have been rather <u>tied up</u> of late! (Sorry about that, I promise I will <u>knot</u> do that again!) (Sorry again!!).

If you recall, you requested some diagrams of the new knots I have been tying. However, would it be better, perhaps, to send you a selection of the physical knots themselves, which I have made in a number of different materials?

Perhaps you could indicate which of these (knotted) materials you would like to receive:

1) 'Laboski Knot' (made in rope)
2) 'Greftarium Knot (made in mouse candle)
3) 'The Sinner Knot' (made in piece of feathered muslin gauze)
4) 'Bravissimo 1000 Knot' (made in tempered steel)
5) 'Mini Pencil Knot' (made in silver/potassium expranite)
6) 'Dr Fischer's Ideology Knot' (made in coloured tissue)
7) 'Fenton Knot' (made in solitary strand of vole hair)

I do hope this is of use, however if you would still prefer diagrams, I would be pleased to assist.

I look forward to hearing from you.

Best wishes,

Robin Cooper

March 1st, 2005, Tuesday

Mr. Robin Cooper
Brondesbury Villas
London
United Kingdom

Dan Lehman
Chanel Terrace, #T-1
Falls Church VA
U.S.A.

Dear Mr. Cooper:

Your letter of 4 October 2004 to Nigel Harding was forwarded to me for my input, by Nigel, as I am frequently involved in correspondence regarding "new" knots. I am sorry for my delay in responding.

You wrote concerning seven knots or knot designs that you have produced. My inference from your letter is that these are *decorative* rather than *practical* knots. Nigel was not sure quite what to do regarding your offer of presenting *physical* (!) examples of them, as we are accustomed to receiving visual images (paper or electronic). You offered to work up some diagrams, if needed; I think that indeed this would be helpful. Perhaps you could also provide some photographs of your work? We might like to publish that, for others to behold, in our quarterly newsletter, *Knotting Matters*. (Though how you go about photographing a knot "made in a solitary strand of Mole hair" will be your challenge—that sounds infinitesimal!!) Your variety of worked materials is fascinating, although some sound as though they might not travel so well. It will be good if some nice images of these can be produced.

Thank you for your interest & offer,
we look forward to seeing what you have wrought.

Sincerely,

R. Danford Lehman
IGKT New-Knot Claims Assessment Committee

Robin Cooper
Brondesbury Villas
London, England

R Danford Lehman
IGKT (International Guild of Knot Tyers) New Knot-Claims Assessment Committee
Chanel Terrace, #T-1
Falls Church VA
USA / America

8th March 2005

Dear Danford,

Let me commence by saying how THRILLED I was to receive such a delightful and charming letter from a verifiable Atlantic cousin.

And so to you may I greet you with a traditional English greeting…

Albion greetings dear friend of mine,
From this land yonder, to thy land beyonder,
O Albion the sweet, Albion the brave,
Do smile kindly 'pon this 'McTavitave'.

You are welcome!

And now to the nitty gritty. You graciously asked me to send you photographs of my seven new knots, which I was delighted to learn that that was what you wanted to receive.

Nay sadly, Danford, I recently suffered a brutal burglarly by some (unknown) oafs who stole not only mine and mine wife's valuable possessions (including her ankle support-couplings), but my entire knot collection, sketches and photographs.

So depressed have I been of late, that I have taken to wandering aimlessly around our local park, pausing only to sob before the (totally uninquisitive) swans, as they softly swim in gentle circles round the shimmering millpond.

However your letter really cheered me up! So please find enclosed some sketches, made from memory, of my seven, new knots. You will note that I have used my own method of labeling.

I do hope you like them. Do let me know.

All the billy best of British,

Robin Cooper
PS – Please excuse the quality of my sketches. I have had to draw them 'pon a desecrated desk.

Robin Cooper's Seven (7) New Knots.

① LABOSKI KNOT (ROPE)

North tendency

Whiting

Watling

② GREETARIUM KNOT (MOUSE CANDLE)

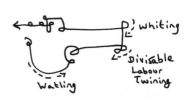

Whiting

Divisable Labour Twining

Watling

③ THE SINNER KNOT (FEATHERED MUSLIN)

whiting

Slippage Trussing

Watling

④ BRAVISSIMO 100 KNOT (TEMPERED STEEL)

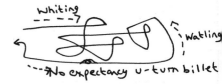

Whiting

Watling

No expectancy u-turn billet

⑤ MINI PENCIL KNOT (SILVER/POTASSIUM EXPRANITE)

whiting

Watling

⑥ DR FISCHER'S IDEOLOGY KNOT (COLOURED TISSUE

Watling

Desized hook-loo

whiting

⑦ FENTON KNOT (SOLITARY VOLE HAIR)

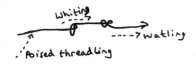

whiting

Watling

Poised threadling

END OF CORRESPONDENCE

Robin Cooper
Brondesbury Villas
London

Tom Sinclair
Honorary Secretary
The Long Distance Walkers Association Ltd
High Street
Wrotham
Sevenoaks
Kent

2nd July 2004

Dear Mr Sinclair,

I am very interested in going on a good old fashioned long distance walk.

Unfortunately, I have no companion who shares the same interest. My wife does not care for walking, and besides, her bad ankle always gets in the way. My neighbour, Peter La Rosse, prefers to sit indoors all the time, fixing his bathroom cabinet – and I can hardly ask Parmaynu!

Anyway, I was wondering if you yourself would care to join me for a long distance walk.

I am planning on walking from London to Sheffield some time in August. The route is actually quite scenic and along the way we will pass the heated windmills along the St Mary estuary, as well as the famous garden bird cemetery at Lime Lim Lim.

Do let me know – it will be lots of fun.

Many thanks in the meantime.

Fingers crossed!

Best wishes,

Robin Cooper

aim: to further the interests of those who enjoy long distance walking

President: Sir John Johnson KCMG

HIGH STREET, WROTHAM, SEVENOAKS, KENT

27th July 2004

Robin Cooper Esq.
Brondesbury Villas
London

Dear Mr. Cooper,

I must apologise for my discourtesy in not responding promptly to your letter of 2nd July. I was pleased to receive your invitation but unable to accept it so what I did, not too presumptuously I trust, was to ask our Editor to insert a brief paragraph in the August issue of our journal, Strider, inviting any interested members to write to you. Strider will be out any minute now so you may receive one or two letters from LDWA members. I enclose a leaflet about our handbook of Long Distance Paths and a Membership Form.

Yours sincerely,

Tom Sinclair, Chairman
c.c. Julie Welch

Robin Cooper
Brondesbury Villas
London

Tom Sinclair
Honorary Secretary
The Long Distance Walkers Association Ltd
High Street
Wrotham
Sevenoaks
Kent

29th July 2004

Dear Mr Sinclair,

Many thanks indeed for your charming letter of two days previous.

I was saddened to hear that you will be unable to join me on my walk, but honoured to hear that you have put a paragraph all about me in your newsletter, 'Spider'.

I enclose £10 for membership herewith. Would you be so kind as to send me the August issue of Spider, as I would very much like to see my name in print!!!!!!

In the meantime, I look forward to receiving letters from fellow Spiders!!!!!!!

Best wishes,

Robin Cooper

LONG DISTANCE WALKERS ASSOCIATION

aim: to further the interests of those who enjoy long distance walking

President: Sir John Johnson KCMG

HIGH STREET, WROTHAM, SEVENOAKS, KENT

3rd August 2004

Robin Cooper Esq.
Brondesbury Villas
London

Dear Mr. Cooper

Thank you for your letter and £10 subscription. I have paid the money into the bank and sent on your form to the Membership Secretary whom I have also asked to send you copies of the April and August Striders. The latter has just come out and I am sorry to say that your address is shown incorrectly in the last minute insertion on page 112. I can only express my regrets for this error and suggest that you explain matters to your neighbour and, if you would be so kind, convey my apologies for any inconvenience caused by the LDWA's regrettable mistake.

Yours sincerely,

Tom Sinclair, Chairman

c.c.s Julie Welch
Garfield Southall

116

Robin Cooper
Brondesbury Villas
London

The Right Honourable Prime Minister Mr Tony Blair
10 Downing Street
London
SW1 2AA

3rd July 2004

Dear Right Honourable Sir,

I understand that you are, of course, a very busy man, and are probably way too busy
to read and re-read this letter.

Nonetheless, I hope that you will take a few minutes – and at the most, an hour - to consider my
idea.

You see, the very fact that you are so <u>busy</u> is what my letter, herewin, concerns.

I put to you, thus, Prime Minister:

What happens when you go to sleep?

In other words, whilst you slumber, the nation still keeps going. Thus, who, in effect, is running
the country?

In short, no one is. No one at all!!!

My idea would be this. Have <u>two</u> Prime Ministers – one for the day, and one for the night.

What do you think? Can we push this through Parliament? Or do I need to fill in a special form
first?

I look forward to hearing from you.

Best wishes,

Robin Cooper

1O DOWNING STREET
LONDON SW1A 2AA

From the Direct Communications Unit   14 July 2004

Mr Robin Cooper
Brondesbury Villas
London

Dear Mr Cooper

The Prime Minister has asked me to thank you for your
recent letter.

Mr Blair was pleased to have your comments, which will be
carefully considered.

Yours sincerely

AEMER LODHI

Robin Cooper
Brondesbury Villas
London

The Right Honourable Prime Minister Mr Tony Blair
10 Downing Street
London
SW1 2AA

27th July 2004

Dear Right Honourable Sir,

Many thanks for replying to my letter. Please pass on my thanks to Aemer Lodhi for physically typing up your response. For your convenience, I have enclosed a copy of the correspondence thus far.

I was delighted to learn that you are considering my idea of two Prime Ministers (one for the day and one for the night). I have since been working up the idea and am pleased to be able to present a pictoral representation of the plan, which I have included along with this letter that you are now reading.

I trust this will be of use.

So Tony, how do we take this to the next level? A meeting?

I look forward to hearing from/meeting with you.

With very best wishes,

Your humble servant,

Robin Cooper

<u>Pictoral Representation of the 'Two Prime Ministers' Plan</u>
By Robin Cooper

① 12:00pm
Tony Blair is Prime Minister (PM)

Early lunch with Industrialists and tennis players, at no. 10 Downing Street

② 3:00pm

Meeting with Greek Ambassador to disc Drachma, and latest livestock figures

③ 4:30pm

Afternoon tea (alone).

④ 6:00pm

Phone call to South African President (tin difference is roughly the same, and the are some cheap rates around at the mom

⑤ 8:00pm

Dinner with Queen and King of Denmark.

⑥ 11:00pm

Prayers and preparation for bed (or 'cot beddie' as Tony Blair calls

PM2

Well, good luck!

Tony Blair

...ne Minister 2 (PM2) enters Tony's bedroom. ...ey formally shake hands. PM2 is now PM.

⑧ 3:00am

US President

PM2

Tell him I'm out!

PM2 makes phone call to US President (due to time difference). Tony Blair is asleep at this time (in his 'cot beddie').

6:00am

PM2

Hello.

Hello.

...holds talks with postmen, milkmen ...early risers. Tony Blair is still ...eep (in his 'cot beddie')

⑩ 9:00am

PM2

'Yawn'

Tax

PM2 has meeting with Cabinet re tax dividends and cuts in the Plastics Industries. Tony Blair is now awake.

Midday (12:00pm)

PM2

Your turn now!

Thanks

Tony Blair

...2 formally shakes hands with ...ny Blair.

⑫ 12:01pm

I'm back, and working for Britain!

Tony Blair (PM)

Tony Blair is PM once again. PM2 goes to bed (or 'cot beddibize' as he calls it).

END OF CORRESPONDENCE

121

Robin Cooper
Brondesbury Villas
London

Pamela Taylor
Chief Executive
Water UK
Queen Anne's Gate
London SW1H 9BT

3rd July 2004

Dear Pamela,

I have an idea that, I believe, could really help the entire British water industry, and the promotion of British water – the finest in the world.

It is so simple, so unique, so clever, (even though I say so myself), that I am surprised no one has ever thought of it.

Would you be interested in hearing more? I'm sure you would!

I very much look forward to hearing from you.

Keep up the good work.

With very best wishes,

Robin Cooper

08 July 2004

WATER UK

Queen Anne's Gate
London
SW1H 9BT

Robin Cooper
Brondesbury Villas
London

Pamela Taylor
Chief Executive

Dear Robin

Many thanks for your letter to our Chief Executive Pamela Taylor on the 03 July. Unfortunately we have been unable to contact you as we do not have your telephone number. May I suggest that you contact Phillip Mills our Director of Water Services to discuss your idea.

Kind regards

Melanie Ogram

EUREAU

INVESTOR IN PEOPLE
Registered Office as above
Registered in England Number 3539600

123

Robin Cooper
Brondesbury Villas
London

Phillip Mills
Director of Water Services
Water UK
Queen Anne's Gate
London SW1H 9BT

12th July 2004

Dear Phillip,

As you can see from the enclosed correspondence, I wrote to Pamela Taylor, Chief Executive, on 3rd July 2004. I received a letter on the 10th of July, dated 8th July, from Melanie Ogram, stating that she was thanking me for my letter, and also that I should give your good self (Phillip Mills) a phone call.

That is why I am writing to you, as I do not own a phone.

Phillip, I have an amazing new idea which, I feel, could revolutionise British Water.

It really is that good.

Would you be interested to hear more about it (the idea)?

I do look forward to hearing from you.

Best wishes,

Robin Cooper

Robin Cooper

14 July 2004

Queen Anne's Gate
London
SW1H 9BT

Robin Cooper
Brondesbury Villas
London

Pamela Taylor
Chief Executive

Dear Robin

I possibly should have explained this in my last letter to you but I actually work for Phillip Mills as his assistant and that is why I am writing to you. If you would be so kind as to send us information about your idea Phillip Mills could have a look at it and reply back to you.

Kind regards

Melanie Ogram
Programme Co-ordinator

INVESTOR IN PEOPLE
Registered Office as above
Registered in England Number 3539600

EUREAU

125

Robin Cooper
Brondesbury Villas
London

Melanie Ogram
Programme Co-ordinator
Water UK
Queen Anne's Gate
London SW1H 9BT

27th July 2004

Dear Melanie,

I trust you remember me:

1) I wrote to Pamela Taylor, Chief Executive, on 3rd July.
2) I receive a letter on the 10th of July, dated 8th July, from your good self.
3) I do not own a phone.
4) I write to Phillip Mills on 12th July.
5) You write to me on 14th July.
6) I receive your letter on 17th July.
7) I write this letter on 27th July.

Phew! We got through that!

As you no doubt now recall, I have an amazing idea that could change the way we use water forever. I believe it would be of paramount benefit for your company (Water UK).

In order for me to fully explain the idea, I would appreciate a meeting. I will be bringing along my own modified water tank, (measuring 10 metres x 12 metres x 7 metres), so I shall need to know the following:

1) Do you have a meeting room sufficiently large enough for my tank?
2) Do you have an 'input/output' water mains pipe?
3) Will you be able to provide towels?

Many thanks for all your help so far.

I look forward to hearing from you.

Best wishes,

Robin Cooper

Robin Cooper

03 August 2004

Mr Robin Cooper
Brondesbury Villas
London

WATER UK

Queen Anne's Gate
London
SW1H 9BT

Pamela Taylor
Chief Executive

Dear Mr Cooper

Thank you for your latest letter of 27 July.

I would like to discuss this with you on the phone but as that is not possible I suggest you come along to our office and we can talk further.

I am just about to go on two weeks holiday so I will not be able to see you until late August.

At the moment I have the following dates/times available:
23 August 11:00 – 12:00
24 August 2:00 – 3:00
25 August 11:00 – 12:00
31 August 3:00 – 4:00

Perhaps you could confirm with my colleague, Melanie Ogram, at this address which date you would prefer.

I am afraid we have no facility to accommodate a tank of the size you mention. This would in fact hold almost 1000 tonnes of water so I wonder if there is a typo in your letter.

I look forward to seeing you and hearing of your idea later this month.

Yours sincerely

Phillip Mills
Director of Water Services

EUREAU

INVESTOR IN PEOPLE
Registered Office as above
Registered in England Number 3539600

Robin Cooper
Brondesbury Villas
London

Phillip Mills
Director of Water Services
Water UK
Queen Anne's Gate
London SW1H 9BT

13th August 2004

Dear Phillip,

Hearty thanks for your letter of 3rd August. I must apologise for taking so long to get back to you - my wife has been rather unwell of late, because of a recurring ankle problem.

But please do not let that worry you.

In the meantime, I trust you have enjoyed a wonderful holiday. Unfortunately, my wife and I have had to cancel ours, due to the aforementioned problem (ankle).

That aside, I would very much like to meet with you. I can do so on 31st August at 3:00. However, I must insist on bringing my modified water tank.

You mentioned in your previous letter that you have 'no facility to accommodate a tank of that (this) size'. Also, you were quite correct in noting that the dimensions of my tank were incorrect. The tank is actually slightly larger than I mentioned, measuring 10 metres x 12 metres x <u>17</u> metres. However, I wonder if you have an outside area, such as a car park, or even a dessication zone, suitable for my tank?

Luckily, I do possess a motorised crane system (which I have adapted to fit my needs), and so would be able to steer the tank into such an area, should you have one.

I would appreciate it if you could let me know if this is still possible. I would call you, but unfortunately I am unable to use the phone, for a variety of reasons*.

I look forward to hearing from you.

Best wishes,

Robin Cooper

Robin Cooper

* Sadly, these are rather private.

19 August 2004

WATER UK

Queen Anne's Gate
London
SW1H 9BT

Mr Robin Cooper
Brondesbury Villas
London

Pamela Taylor
Chief Executive

Dear Mr Cooper

Thank you for your latest letter of the 13 August.

I am able to meet you on the 31st August but we have no car park or other area here in central London where you could construct a tank of the size you mention.

I suggest therefore we meet to discuss the outline and principles of your idea. If you have any drawings or photographs then this would obviously help. I hope his is an acceptable way forward. Perhaps you can confirm with my PA, Melanie Ogram.

Yours sincerely

Phillip Mills
Director of Water Services

EUREAU

INVESTOR IN PEOPLE
Registered Office as above
Registered in England Number 3539600

129

Robin Cooper
Brondesbury Villas
London

Phillip Mills
Director of Water Services
Water UK
Queen Anne's Gate
London SW1H 9BT

29th August 2004

Dear Phillip,

Severe thanks for your letter of 19th August.

I was thrilled to hear that you were able to meet me on the 31st August, however, as I only received your letter this Saturday*, and today now being Bank Holiday Monday, I cannot see how this letter, which I am writing, will get to you in time to alert you as to whether I will/will not be able to make the 31st (which is a Tuesday).

As a matter of fact I can make the Tuesday meeting, but realistically this letter will probably reach you on Wednesday (i.e. a day later), and so I can only see three options:

1) I turn up unexpectedly on Tuesday (but this will now be in the past for you as you will be reading this on the Wednesday, having unexpectedly met me).
2) I don't turn up on Tuesday (this will also be in the past for you, and you will also realise this, from the fact that I wasn't there).
3) We re-arrange.

I think a re-arrangement (option 3) would be the best option.

I will also be happy to bring along any sketches, swatches and swadlings, where necessary.

Please accept my utmost apologies for the potential re-arrangement.

In the meantime I look forward to hearing from you.

In yours, I remain,

Robin Cooper

* I can only assume this was due to a mix-up in the post office. Do you wish me to contact them on your behalf? Would you also be prepared to offer an affi-david, if asked?

7 September 2004

Mr Robin Cooper
Brondesbury Villas
London

Queen Anne's Gate
London
SW1H 9BT

Pamela Taylor
Chief Executive

Dear Mr Cooper

Many thanks for your letter but I am afraid due to the length of time this correspondence has taken and a busy schedule at the moment we will no longer be able to continue to correspond with you on this matter.

Kind regards

Melanie Ogram

END OF CORRESPONDENCE

EUREAU

INVESTOR IN PEOPLE
Registered Office as above
Registered in England Number 3539600

131

Robin Cooper
Brondesbury Villas
London

The Chairman (couldn't find the name)
MENSA
St John's Square
Wolverhampton
WV2 4AH

5th July 2004

Dear Sir/Madam,

I am honoured to be writing to such a clever man, in charge of such a clever organisation – an organisation DEVOTED to the furtherance of the cleverest people in this fayre land of ours.

That said, let me now give you your starter for 10...

Which European financial administrator declared "Je waarden teca monaten hem taavel The Beatles?"

Correct, the answer is..... (Answer at the bottom of the page)!

What I am trying to say is, I am an amateur quiz-master and enjoy nothing more than writing quizzes, then setting them for friends, family and colleagues. Whether it be for money or mere reputation, nothing quite beats a quiz – except perhaps a holiday abroad!!!!

I am currently planning on holding the world's largest quiz (literally – you'll see why in a few words...), featuring people over 7 feet tall. (Now do you see?).

The event – 'Think Big 2004' - will be held in my local civic centre towards the end of the year, and I am hoping to gather at least 200 seven feet quiz fans – from all over Britain.

Would MENSA care to sponsor me? I am looking to raise £65,000. In exchange I would be prepared to become MENSA's in-house quiz master, setting your members their own, free, personal quiz questions for a period of 5 years.

I look forward to hearing from you.

Best wishes,

R. Li C. ~

Robin Cooper

Answer: Trick question. In actual fact the administrator was the Chinese economist, Lin Hua Xing, but he was speaking through a European interpreter.

Mensa
The High IQ Society

British Mensa Limited
St. John's Square
Wolverhampton
WV2 4AH

Mr R Cooper
Brondesbury Villas
London

6th July 2004

Dear Mr Cooper

Thank you for your letter to the Chairman.

Your project is a very interesting idea and may well capture people's imaginations. Mensa however is already heavily committed on future projects and would not be able to support the activity you are proposing at this time.

We do however wish you every success with the idea.

Yours sincerely,

John Stevenage.
Chief Executive.

norary President, *Sir Clive Sinclair*

A Meeting Of Minds

133

Robin Cooper
Brondesbury Villas
London

John Stevenage
Chief Executive
MENSA
St John's Square
Wolverhampton
WV2 4AH

11th July 2004

Dear Mr Stevenage,

I was honoured to receive a letter from your good slef on the 8th July (although you wrote yours on the 6th).

First of all, I am terribly sorry that I did not address my previous letter to you in name, and do trust I have not dented your (good) reputation (nor mine, in thine eyes!).

Also, I should very much like to thank you for saying my idea is "interesting". You cannot know how much that meant to me – or my wife. Thank you again – from the both of us.

I am sorry that you did not feel that my idea ('Think Big 2004') was quite right for you or MENSA. However, I do have a solution: I am prepared to change the name of the event to, 'Think MENSA Big 2004'.

Interested now….? Then read on….

All the participants in 'Think MENSA Big 2004' will be specially chosen from the ranks of MENSA itself. All you would need to do is supply those members - men and women - who attain a height of 7 feet and more.

I have already started work on the logo and merchandise ('Think MENSA Big 2004' balloons, coffee mugs, blow heaters etc). It's all very exciting.

So – are you in?

I look forward to hearing from you again.

All the best.

R. Li C.

Robin Cooper

Mensa
The High IQ Society

British Mensa Limited
St. John's Square
Wolverhampton
WV2 4AH

Mr R Cooper
Brondesbury Villas
London

15th July 2004

Dear Mr Cooper

Thank you for your letter of 11th July and the suggestion of the Think Mensa Big 2004.

Mensa already has a programme of competitions and games that involve members. We would not, therefore, look for further involvement in any other event at this time.

Thank you for thinking of us though.

Yours sincerely,

John Stevenage.
Chief Executive.

END OF CORRESPONDENCE

Robin Cooper
Brondesbury Villas
London

H E Price
Honorary General Secretary
The British Caravanners Club
Westwood Way
Coventry
Warks

13th July 2004

Dear H E Price,

I send thee this letter from one caravan ENTHUSIAST to another! Welcome brother.

I am writing to you for your help on a small problem I have.

I recently returned from a short caravanning break in Guildford with my wife.

Whilst we were travelling back home on the motorway, the bit that connects the car to the caravan (I forget the technical name), came away and the caravan crashed into the motorway barrier, ricocheted off, bounced around a bit, then rolled down a hill and burst into FLAMES like in a film.

Needless to say we were completely distraught, not least because my wife had left her favourite apron (she's had it for over 10 years) inside the caravan. I searched amongst the burnt out wreckage but sadly all that was left of her apron was a burnt out pouch.

I wonder if your society would be prepared to replace my wife's apron. She is really lost without it, and what with her bad ankle, it only makes her more irritable.

I'll describe the apron to you: on it was a picture of 'Greville the Green Finch' with the words, 'My wife sings for her supper' emblazened across it. It was in cream and brown (standard size). I believe you can buy it in most kitchen centres.

I really don't like to beg, but I feel you're my last recourse. Will you help, O' brother?

I look forward to your reply.

Kindest of regards,

Robin Cooper

BRITISH CARAVANNERS CLUB

SECTION OF THE CAMPING AND CARAVANNING CLUB

Reg. Office: Westwood Way, Coventry CV4 8JH

PATRON
H.R.H. The Duke of Edinburgh
K.G. K.T.

PRESIDENT

Don Geeson

3675/dell/r10
Robin Cooper
Brondesbury Villas
London

July 17th 2004

Dear Robin Cooper,

I received by this mornings mail your letter dated July 13th 2004 forwarded to me by Camping and Caravanning Club Headquarters.

I much regret the accident to your caravan and also the loss of your wife's special apron.

Unfortunately we have no facility allowing us to replace the apron and respectfully suggest you contact your insurers.

I hope your caravan is not a write off and you will shortly be able to caravan again.

Yours sincerely,

Herbert Price.
Honorary General Secretary.

END OF CORRESPONDENCE

137

Robin Cooper
Brondesbury Villas
London

David Parkin
Chairman
The British Hat Guild
c/o Parkin Fabrics Ltd
Vulcan Street
Oldham
Lancs

1st August 2004

Dear Mr Parkin,

I have enjoyed immense success as a milliner (hat maker) across the continent, and in particular, Belgium. Until now, I have perhaps rather shunned the British hat industry for reasons, shall we say, of *ignoblesse de petit pertinence*!

However, I am now ready to cast off my wicked aspersions and have set a date for my first UK gala hat show – 'Superhat Now. Superhat Then. Superhat When?'.

'Superhat Now. Superhat Then. Superhat When?' will feature some of my most famed hats, plus hat-related events, including (and here's where you come in), a talk given by your good self, on the state of the British hat industry.

Would you care to take part? The date is fixed for Saturday October 2nd. The place – Windsor Castle (TBC).

I enclose an invite.

I do hope you will be there.

With best wishes,

Robin Cooper

David Parkin Esq.

You are invited to:

SUPERHAT NOW. SUPERHAT THEN. SUPERHAT WHEN?

A Celebration of Robin Cooper's fine millinery and the great British hat

Windsor Castle, Windsor, Berkshire, SL4 (TBC)
Saturday 2nd October 2004
7am – 6pm

Admission £16 adults, £11 children, £8 OAP's
(£2 discount for hat wearers)

Featuring:

Live Discussion hosted by Robin Cooper

'Where Now?' - A talk on the state of the British hat industry by
David Parkin, Chairman, the British Hat Guild

Childrens' (hat) rides

♫ Music by Paul & Bridget Santini-Henderson

And much more...

It's the **biggest** hat event of the year...!

Invite no. 00136

139

the british hat guild

Mr Robin Cooper
Brondesbury Villas
London

10 August 2004

Dear Mr Cooper

Thank you very much for the invite to your Hat event.

As this would mean a special trip for me please advise if you would be willing to pay
overnight and travel expenses.

On a practical note, should you decide to set up in business as a milliner here in
England then as the largest supplier of fabrics for ladies hats in the UK, we would be
happy to supply you.

Looking forward to hearing from you.

Yours sincerely,

DF Parkin
Chairman

Robin Cooper
Brondesbury Villas
London

David Parkin
Chairman
The British Hat Guild
c/o Parkin Fabrics Ltd
Vulcan Street
Oldham
Lancs

13th August 2004

Dear Mr Parkin,

I received your letter of respondence of 10th August, for which I am eternally grateful.

In addition, I was thrilled that you were reserving your place for the event ('Superhat Now. Superhat Then. Superhat When?') – it's gonna be great!

You enquired as to whether I would be willing to pay for your overnight and travel expenses. That is of course no problem at all.

My driver, Louis de la Ville, will be able to collect you from your business or home address, and drive you to London (although you may have to share part of the journey with his wife and children).

Regarding accommodation, there is ample room at a wonderful, local guest house, of which I am co-partner. 'The Yuletide Expression' offers de luxe double bedrooms/suites plus an all night hockey pitch, should you require practice.

Regarding your talk at the event ('Where Now?' – a discourse on the state of the British hat industry), would you be willing to send me a draft of your speech prior to the event? I trust a 40 minute piece would suffice?

In the meantime, I will spread the word that you will be there (this will really help ticket sales), and I look forward to hearing from you.

Best wishes,

Robin Cooper

END OF CORRESPONDENCE

Robin Cooper
Brondesbury Villas
London

Yvonne Orgill
Secretary
The Bathroom Manufacturers Association
Station Road
Stoke-on-Trent
Staffs

3rd August 2004

Dear Yvonne,

Allow myself to introduce me…

I currently hold the British record for cleaning and polishing bathtubs (98 tubs in 2 hours, 16 minutes, 44 seconds).

Would you care to do a feature on me in your newsletter? I have many fascinating stories to tell. I have even been on Belgian television – twice!

With very best wishes,

R. L. C

Robin Cooper

Mr. Robin Cooper

Brondesbury Villas

London

THE BATHROOM
MANUFACTURERS
ASSOCIATION

Dear Mr Cooper,

Yvonne has passed your letter detailing your accomplishments onto me, the Marketing Manager for the secretariat. It was good to hear about your achievements, and we're willing to enter you into our association news that is sent out to our 38 member companies. All we need is a bit more information on your British record and television appearances. A general who, what, why, where, when and how should be enough.

Many thanks and kind regards,

Jason Saunt

Marketing Manager

Robin Cooper
Brondesbury Villas
London

Jason Saunt
Marketing Manager
The Bathroom Manufacturers Association
Station Road
Stoke-on-Trent
Staffs

12th August 2004

Dear Jason,

Many thanks for your kind letter. I was delighted to hear that you were interested in including a piece about me in your association newsletter.

So – where do I start…? Well, at the beginning I suppose!

I have been involved (on a semi-permanent on/off basis), in the bathroom world for many years, and have always prided myself on keeping any bathtub I come into contact with, spotless.

My reputation soon preceded me. So much so that one day, a Belgian colleague of mine (Henrig Thomas Van Heederstaandtsig), suggested I enter the annual bathtub cleaning contest in Belgium (known as 'Baddi Van Huis Ghen Hebitge').

And so, on December 9th 1999, I found myself in the village of Duitsliinge, 20 miles from Haavenhilps, as the only British competitor in Baddi Van Huis Ghen Hebitge. My task was to clean and polish 98 bath tubs in as short as time as possible. In addition, I was only allowed a small piece of cotton rag and three bars of soap to work with. As you can imagine, it was a pretty tense time, as there were over 5,000 spectators in the arena, and all of this was being filmed for Belgian television.

Much to my surprise, I beat the favourite (A Spaniard named Luis Jorginas), and finished in first place, with a time of 2 hours, 16 minutes, 44 seconds. Much to my delight, I was also awarded a cash prize equal to about £160,000.

So, that's my story! Will you print it?

In the meantime, I wish you well.

Best wishes,

Robin Cooper

Robin Cooper

END OF CORRESPONDENCE

144

Robin Cooper
Brondesbury Villas
London

Peter Hybart
Executive Director
Tennis Whales
National Tennis Centre
Ocean Park
Cardiff
CF1 5HF

18th August 2004

Dear Mr Hybart,

I wonder if you can help me…

I recently overheard someone talking about your organisation ('Tennis Whales'), and felt I just had to write.

Could you please tell me - as it's driving me mad - what exactly are 'tennis whales'? And if they are what I assume (i.e whales that can somehow play tennis), is there really an organisation devoted to them?

I would be grateful if you could put me out of my misery.*

I look forward to hearing from you.

Best wishes,

Robin Cooper

* I might also win a bet!

TENNIS WALES
TENIS CYMRU

Tennis Wales
Welsh National Tennis Centre,
Ocean Way, Ocean Park, Cardiff CF24 5HF

Executive Director – P. Hybart

As you see - the spelling you have is incorrect. We are the governing body for Tennis within Wales. Wales being part of the U.K.

Sponsors of Welsh Tennis Development
British Polythene Industries • DR Cecil Jones & Son Ltd • Edwards Geldard • Konica Peter Llewellyn Ltd
Mercedes Benz (UK) Ltd • Sportsmatch • Sunjuice Ltd • Wilson Sporting Goods

END OF CORRESPONDENCE

Robin Cooper
Brondesbury Villas
London

Paul Talboys
Chief Executive
The Bingo Association
High Street North
Dunstable
Beds

9th November 2004

Dear Mr Talboys,

I have recently been left with 600 kilogrammes of herring, and I have absolutely no idea what to do with it all.

My wife is going mad, as she is unable to use the living room (the herrings are lying in sacks on the floor), and I am concerned that the fish may start going off within a week or two.

I wonder if you would consider in taking it off me? I thought you might be interested, as you could give it out as a prize at one of your many Bingo halls.

Does this idea appeal?

I look forward to herring from you.

Best wishes,

Robin Cooper

THE NATIONAL GAME

17ᵗʰ November 2004

The National Bingo Game Association Ltd
High Street North
Dunstable
Beds

Mr Robin Cooper
Brondesbury Villas
London

Dear Mr Cooper

Thank you for your recent letter regarding surplus herring.

Regrettably there are very strict guidelines on the use of herring as prizes in bingo clubs. Can I suggest that you contact your nearest pet food manufacturer and ask if they could make use of any surplus fish your wife is unable to utilise.

In the meantime, I wish you luck in your efforts – you may need it!

Yours sincerely

Paul Talboys
Chief Executive

END OF CORRESPONDENCE

147

Robin Cooper
Brondesbury Villas
London

David Sparkes
Chief Executive
The Amateur Swimming Association
Derby Sq
Loughborough
Leics
LE11 5AL

10th November 2004

Dear Mr Sparkes,

I am planning on swimming the English Channel as a surprise for my wife.

She loves surprises and she loves swimming and she loves the Channel and she loves me (I hope!), so all in all everyone wins!

However, I can't swim.

I am hoping that once I get in the water, the desire to succeed at all costs will propel me to victory, or rather, *victoire*. Do you think this is feasible?*

Ideally I would like to set off within three to four weeks. Any advice?

Many thanks,

Robin Cooper

* Sadly, I do not know the French for 'feasible'.

FOUNDED: 1869
PATRON: H.M. THE QUEEN

Chief Executive's Office

Ref: ds/js

17 November 2004

Mr R Cooper
Brondesbury Villas
London

Dear Mr Cooper

I acknowledge receipt of your letter dated 10 November 2004 and feel the best advice I can offer is to suggest that you look for another surprise for your wife. To swim the Channel requires training, skill and above all good luck. I fear if you are unable to swim it is unlikely in 4 weeks you will have the skill or background training to attempt this crossing. There are specialist organisations who can advise you on preparing for such a swim but I think you are a little away from that at the moment. Perhaps your initial goal should be to surprise you wife by simply swimming.

Yours sincerely

David Sparkes
Chief Executive

END OF CORRESPONDENCE

HEAD OFFICE: DERBY SQUARE LOUGHBOROUGH LE11 5AL

149

Robin Cooper
Brondesbury Villas
London

Maggie Loughran
Administrator
The Federation of Family History Societies
PO Box 2425
Coventry
Warks

11th November 2004

Dear Maggie Loughran,

I stumbled across your organisation by pure chance* but boy am I happy to hear from you!

I understand you are devoted to the bringing together of societies relating to family history. It is with this knowledge that I am writing to you, as I believe your society (and indeed your fellow societies) will be interested in the following information that I am just about to write...

When I was a mere scamp, my father would tell me many wonderful stories all about his grandfather, (my great grandfather) (also called Robin Cooper)).

Robin Cooper was a leading philanthropist in the 19th century. During his life-time he set up a number of drop-in-centres, where the poor, orphaned, or merely misguided could enjoy a boiled egg with a real silver spoon.

Such a simple gesture was believed to lift the men's spirits.

The centres – known as 'Egg Houses' – ran for 15 years, and in all that time, only one spoon ever went missing. When my great grandfather found the guilty culprit (Edward Minton), he refused to thrash him (as was customary in those days), but merely covered his body in salt. The salt served as a poignant reminder of the bitterness caused through the act of theft. Minton never stole again.

Would you (or indeed the federation's friends/societies) like to hear more of this wonderful man from history yonder?

Best wishes,

Robin Cooper

Robin Cooper

* I overheard your organisation's name whilst at a motorway service station with my wife. The gentleman on the next table but one mentioned your society with the phrase, "Keep the lights on dear Penhaligon". Can you possibly enlighten me as to the origin of this phrase?

150

Robin Cooper
Brondesbury Villas
London

Peter Still
Managing Director
John Lewis Superstore
300 Oxford Street
London W1A 1EX

21st November 2004

Dear Mr Still,

Good tidings to you and all your staff for the festive season ahead (Christmas).

Now to the crux of the matter-in-my-hand:

I am a fully-qualified Santa Claus, and am wondering whether you might consider me to run my own 'Santa's Grotto' in your store.

But WAIT! You're probably thinking: 'what makes him so special?'

Well, first of all, I have made several changes to the characterisation of Father Christmas. Rather than greeting the children with shouts of 'Ho, ho, ho!', I prefer to whisper the phrase 'Dependence is not unfathomable in this cruel world we live in'. In addition, my gifts are ALL hand-made, ranging from felt hoops to vanilla-pod holders.

You will note also, from the enclosed sketch, that I have radically redesigned Santa's outfit, and, in addition, have renamed my character, 'Lord Buckles'.

Would you be interested in employing me? I promise NEVER to let you down.

I look forward to hearing from you.

Best wishes,

Robin Cooper

Robin Cooper

LORD BUCKLES

— see him in his 'Grotto' !!!

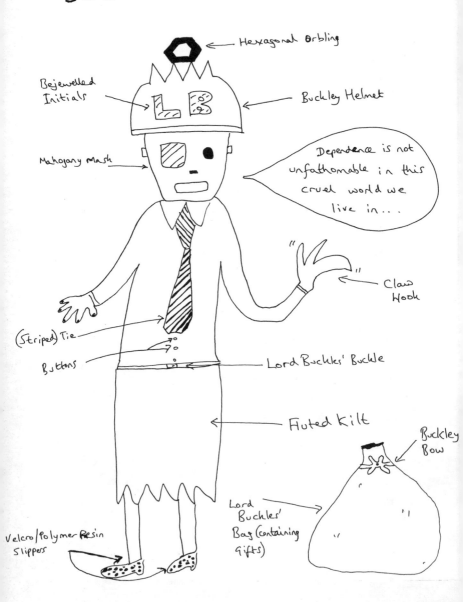

Hexagonal Orbling

Bejewelled Initials

Buckley Helmet

Mahogany Mask

Dependence is not unfathomable in this cruel world we live in...

Claw Hook

(Striped) Tie

Buttons

Lord Buckles' Buckle

Fluted Kilt

Buckley Bow

Lord Buckles' Bag (containing gifts)

Velcro/Polymer Resin Slippers

John Lewis

1 December 2004
PO/JW

Oxford Street

300 Oxford Street
London W1A 1EX

Personal
Mr B Cooper
Brondesbury Villas
London

Dear Mr Cooper

Thank you for your letter regarding possible employment within John Lewis.   I am sorry to be writing to tell you that we do not have a suitable vacancy at present and therefore cannot take your interest further.   I do hope you will not be too disappointed.

Thank you for the time and trouble you have taken with your application.

Yours sincerely

J. West

Jean West
Personnel

The John Lewis Partnership

John Lewis plc Registered in England 233462
Registered Office 171 Victoria Street
London SW1E 5NN

153

Robin Cooper
Brondesbury Villas
London

Jean West
Personnel
John Lewis Superstore
300 Oxford Street
London W1A 1EX

Your ref: PO/JW
My ref: KJI 8/90.56/HTUR er6V

5th December 2004

Dear Ms West,

I wonder if you can help.

I wrote to Mr Peter Still on the 21st November, seeking employment as your in-store Santa ('Lord Buckles').

A letter of replyance was then sent – by your good self – to my abode, but addressed to a Mr 'B Cooper'. I, as you can see from the name at the bottom*, am a Mr 'R Cooper'.

By chance, my cousin Barry Cooper was staying with me at the time, and, believing the letter was addressed to him (i.e. Mr B – Barry – Cooper), opened your letter.

Alas, this has caused great problems within my household, as my cousin then showed your letter to my wife. She quizzed me as to the origination of the original letter that provoked your (wrongly addressed) reply, and I had to admit my lifelong secret identity as Lord Buckles.

My wife is very upset as she does not approve of this alter ego, and thus the whole fiasco has caused a worsening of her already poorly ankle.

Would you be prepared to write a short apology letter to my wife (Mrs Cooper)? This would really put my and her mind(s) at rest.

With kind regards,

Robin Cooper (Mr R Cooper*)
PS - Perhaps now you would re-consider my application as your in-store Santa ('Lord Buckles')?

John Lewis

15 December 2004
REC/JW

Oxford Street

300 Oxford Street
London W1A 1EX

Personal
Mr R Cooper
Brondesbury Villas
London

Dear Mr Cooper

Thank you for your letter dated 5 December 2004 pointing out my typing error.   Please accept my apologies for any upset this may have caused.   I have also written to your wife apologising.

With regard to the position as in-store Santa I am sorry to tell you that we already have an in-store Santa and therefore cannot take your interest further.

Yours sincerely

Jean West
Personnel

The John Lewis Partnership

John Lewis plc Registered in England 233462
Registered Office 171 Victoria Street
London SW1E 5NN

155

John Lewis

15 December 2004
REC/JW

www.johnlewis.com

Oxford Street

300 Oxford Street
London WIA IEX

Personal
Mrs Cooper
Brondesbury Villas
London

Dear Mrs Cooper

I am writing to apologise for any upset you may have suffered when a letter, which I incorrectly addressed to Mr B Cooper and not Mr R Cooper, was opened by Mr B Cooper (your husbands's cousin).

Yours sincerely

J. West

Jean West
Personnel

The John Lewis Partnership

John Lewis plc Registered in England 233462
Registered Office 171 Victoria Street
London SWIE 5NN

Robin Cooper
Brondesbury Villas
London

Director
The Science Museum
Exhibition Road
London
SW7 2DD

25th November 2004

Dear Sir/Madam,

Would it be possible for my family and I to celebrate Christmas Day, all alone, in your charming museum?

During our visit I will be giving my family my very own 'Christmas lecture', which will be all about jet aircraft. As this is a practical and 'hands-on' lecture, this will also involve the dismantling of one of your exhibits (probably the Gloster-Whittle E28/39 jet engine, built around 1941).

I promise to be very careful (I shall wear gloves), and to put all the parts back in their correct order straight afterwards.

This would be a real treat for all of the family, and so I do hope this can be arranged.

I look forward to hearing from you.

Best wishes,

Robin Cooper

From the Director
Dr Lindsay Sharp

8 December 2004

Robin Cooper
Brondesbury Villas
London

Dear Robin Cooper

Many thanks for your letter. We are of course always keen to encourage our visitors to develop a close understanding of the wonderful objects in our collections. Visitor research also shows us how important is the role of the adult members of family groups in communicating the significance of objects to younger visitors.

However, I am obliged to tell you that we will not be able to accede to your request. You will understand the serious obligations that the National Heritage Act places on our shoulders in respect to preserving our objects for future generations. Although I'm sure you would take the utmost care if you were to disassemble the Whittle engine, you will understand that this is not something that we could permit.

Also, I'm sure that you understand that similar concerns would apply to our opening on Christmas Day. This is the only day of the year when all but our security staff are absent from the premises, taking a well-earned break. It would be insurmountably expensive for us to open for one group.

May I suggest that, although less vivid than the lecture you propose, you turn to our new website, *Making the Modern World* (http://www.makingthemodernworld.org.uk/). If you enter the word "Whittle" into the search box, you will be able to enjoy a whole narrative on the subject of Frank Whittle and his engine. For more detail, I would recommend you turn to the latest book by my colleague Andrew Nahum, *Frank Whittle: Invention of the Jet* (Icon Books, 2004).

Kind regards

[signature]

Lindsay Sharp

END OF CORRESPONDENCE

Science Museum
Exhibition Road LONDON SW7 2DD

Mr F C Culley
Secretary
The British Domesticated Ostrich Association
Little Corby
Carlisle
Cumbria CA4 8QW

10th February 2005

Dear Mr Culley,

I wonder if you can help.

I am thinking of buying an ostrich (a live one), as a pet, and was planning on keeping him/her in my garden, so that he/she can roam about freely and without a care in the world.

However, I currently own a wild boar who lives in a makeshift dwelling in my garden. Camfy (the name of my boar) is unfortunately quite an unpredictable beast: one minute he is happily gnawing away at his metal pole, the next, tearing great lumps out of our oak tree with his powerful set of teeth.

As a leading expert on ostrii, would you be able to offer me any advice as to which type of ostrich I should buy? Ideally I would need one that could co-exist with Camfy, or at least outrun him.

I look forward to hearing from you and thank you – in advance – for your help,

Best wishes,

Robin Cooper

Camfy, the wild boar.

159

British
Domesticated
Ostrich
Association

R. Cooper, Esq.,
Brondesbury Villas,
London

11th February 2005

Dear Mr. Cooper,

Thank you for your letter of the 10th instant.

I am sure that you will appreciate the BDOA is more involved in the rearing of farmed ostrich rather than ostrich as pets. I would, however, advise against keeping an ostrich as a pet as it is a flock bird and should not be kept in isolation. How an ostrich would cope with Camfy I cannot guess but wonder if either would be safe together as the foot of an ostrich can be dangerous as it has a large 'toe' which could be lethal.

On the other hand you would need a licence to keep ostrich under the Dangerous Wild Animals Act and would have to comply with the requirements of your local authority as regards the conditions under which the bird would need to be kept. At the same time you do not say how big a garden you have as they do need plenty of space within which to exercise. I suspect you would not be granted a licence based on the problems our farming members have.

Yours sincerely,

C. Culley

Secretary

END OF CORRESPONDENCE

LITTLE CORBY, CARLISLE, CA4 8QW.
SECRETARY/TREASURER: CRAIG CULLEY

Robin Cooper
Brondesbury Villas
London

Digby Morgan-Jones
Secretary
The Natural Sausage Casings Association
High Street
Riseley
Beds

24th February 2005

Dear Mr –Jones,

Many thanks for your letter. It was greatly appreciated.

I was pleased to hear you were interested in my project and look forward to our meeting on Monday April 11th at 2pm.

I will of course bring along all the various components, so that you can have a good look for yourself.

Until then,

Best wishes,

Robin Cooper

NSCA
NATURAL SAUSAGE CASING ASSOCIATION

Robin Cooper, Esq.,
Brondesbury Villas
London

28 February 2005

Dear Mr. Cooper

Meeting – Monday 11th April 2005 at 2pm.

I was very surprised to receive your letter of the 26th February 2005, as I have not written to you from this office.

Whether my Chairman or one of the members have written I do not know.

I shall not be meeting you as you indicated, as I know nothing about it.

Yours sincerely

D. Morgan-Jones

Digby Morgan-Jones
Secretary

MEMBER
EUROPEAN NATURAL SAUSAGE CASINGS ASSOCIATION
HAMBURG FRG.

Robin Cooper
Brondesbury Villas
London

David Smith
Chief Executive
The National Association of Master Bakers
Baldock Street
Ware, Herts

16th March 2005

Dear Mr Smith,

I have been baking bread for about 7 years now. I specialize in wholemeal, white, granary, granalium and thantium breads but I am also CAPABLE of baking bespoke bread, should the need arise.

I am currently undertaking a very exciting project, in which I bake life-size models of leading individuals from the baking and bread world, and would be honoured if you would allow me to bake a model of your good self.

I plan to unveil my 'bread portraits' at Southampton Docks in October.

Would this be something you would be keen on doing?

I look forward to hearing from you.

Best wishes,

Robin Cooper

NATIONAL ASSOCIATIC
OF
MASTEI
BAKER!
SERVING THE BAKING COMMUNIT

Robin Cooper
Brondesbury Villas
London

04/04/2005

Dear Robin

Thank you for your interesting letter. I am flattered that you think me worthy
of modelling. I do have a very full diary and before agreeing to your request I
do need to know the time scale and the amount of commitment you would
need from me.

Kind regards

David Smith
Chief Executive
National Association of Masterbakers

Robin Cooper
Brondesbury Villas
London

David Smith
Chief Executive
The National Association of Master Bakers
Baldock Street
Ware, Herts

5th April 2005

Dear Mr Smith,

Many thanks for your letter of 4th April. I was delighted that you were interested in becoming a model.

You asked for some more information, of which I am of course, happy to provide.

I would expect the modelling session to last about 3 hours, during which you would be asked to sit quite still, whilst I fashion you in dough. Should you require short breaks, for toilet or sips of water, then they can be provided. I am happy to carry out the modeling session at your premises or anywhere you may feel comfortable.

I now have a couple of questions to ask you:

1) For extra impact, I have cast my previous models in a number of different costumes. Is there a figure from history or a world leader that you identify with? If so, I would be happy to provide you with their costume.

2) What type of bread would you like to see yourself cast in? I am totally flexible, and can provide just about any kind of dough.

I do hope this helps you make your decision.

I look forward to (fingers crossed) working with you on this exciting project.

Best wishes,

Robin Cooper

DGS/kd

11 April 2005

Mr Robin Cooper
Brondesbury Villas
London

Dear Mr Cooper

Thank you for your letter. My apologies for taking time to get back to you.

Thank you for you kind offer to bake a model of me, the first offer of its kind, unfortunately I am extremely busy at this time, having taken on the running of our training section, as well as the day to day running of the NA.

I would be very interested to see photographs of the bread portraits when they have been made.

Good Luck

David Smith
Chief Executive Officer

END OF CORRESPONDENCE

Robin Cooper
Brondesbury Villas
London

Adrian Holmes
Operations Manager
The National Federation of Retail Newsagents
Sekforde Street
London EC1

18th March 2005

Dear Mr Holmes,

Having been told countless times about the reliability, good-graciousness, and sheer efficiency of your federation, I am writing to you for some advice.

I have recently set up my own newsagents ('Mr Nicker Nose'), from which I work on a part-time basis - the rest of the time the shop is run by a gentleman by the name of Calfer Williams.

Mr Nicker Nose is different from all other newsagents because we do not stock any brands of sweets, chocolate or confect that are sold in any other newsagents in Britain. Everything is completely home-made. We even make our own soft drink – 'Tominto', which is a healthy blend of tomato puree, mint syrup and milk.

As one of the leading figures in newsagency, would you be prepared to accompany me on a three week nationwide press tour to help promote Mr Nicker Nose? I already have several newspapers and radio stations interested. In return, I can pay your travel and accommodation expenses – and offer you unlimited Tominto.

I look forward to hearing from you.

Best wishes,

Robin Cooper

HEAD OFFICE

21st March, 2005

Mr. R. Cooper,
Brondesbury Villas
London

Dear Mr. Cooper,

Thank you for your letter of 18th March 2005.

The Federation is always interested in learning of new and improved ways of enhancing membership value, and therefore I have copied your letter (and this reply) to my Head of Field Operations, Charles Fleckney. Regrettably, I will personally be unable to commit the time you have requested.

Charles will ensure that one of our Field Team get in touch with you over the next few days, to talk things through, and to see how the Federation can be of assistance.

Yours sincerely,

Adrian Holmes
Director of Operations

Representing the Trade in The British Isles and The Republic of Ireland

National Federation of Retail Newsagents
Sekforde Street London EC1

Robin Cooper
Brondesbury Villas
London

Charles Fleckney
Head of Field Operations
The National Federation of Retail Newsagents
Sekforde Street
London EC1

6th April 2005

Dear Mr Fleckney,

Re: Mr Nicker Nose

I trust you have been very busy of late, but wonder if you have had a chance to peruse the contained letters that I believe were passed on to your good slef by Adrian Holmes?

As you now know, Mr Holmes was sadly unable to accompany me on my tour to promote my newsagents, 'Mr Nicker Nose'. I was upset but I did understand.

So Mr Fleckney, I wonder if you would be happy to be my travel companion? I shan't deny that it will be hard work but it will also be a lot of fun, as we will be travelling by as many different forms of transport as possible (train, car, taxi, coach, barge, horse and cart, 'squirrel-magnet', van, ferry) for maximum VISUAL impact .

I firmly believe that this is a great way of putting not just Mr Nicker Nose, but newsagency as a whole on the map - and that's gotta be good for the both of us!

What do you say?

I look forward to hearing from you – hopefully with a resounding 'YES'!

Best wishes,

Robin Cooper

11th April 2005

Mr R Cooper
Brondesbury Villas
London

Dear Mr Cooper,

Further to your recent correspondence with the Federation, I can confirm that I have asked our Retail Development Manager to make contact with you, but we have been unable to ascertain the address of your retail business.

Can you please advise me by return of your shop address, supplying wholesaler and box number so that I can arrange for our Retail Development Manager to make contact with you.

Please note they will not be able to attend a private residential address in the first instance.

Yours sincerely,

PP

Charles Fleckney
National Training and Field Operations Manager

c.c.   Adrian Holmes
        David Greener

Robin Cooper
Brondesbury Villas
London

Charles Fleckney
National Training and Field Operations Manager
The National Federation of Retail Newsagents
Sekforde Street
London EC1

13th April 2005

Dear Mr Fleckney,

Re: Mr Nicker Nose

Many thanks for your letter of two days previous to this one. You asked a couple of questions, to which I am happy to give answers to you.

1) 'Can you (I) please advise me (you) by return of your (my) shop address':
Certainly, I operate from an extended 'platform/billet house' approx. 30 feet above and away from my abode.

2) '...Supplying wholesaler and box number':
Firstly, I shall deal with the wholesaler number:

Regrettably, I am not quite sure which of the following numbers is the correct one, as I have a number of rather complicated forms with lots of numbers on them. It is either:

    a) 145/978881-89/JH.8U 067/6Y/9IU/mM54
    b) 8905-8
    c) 8905-9

Regarding the box number - again I am somewhat confused as to which one this is, as the forms appear to have been mixed up by my colleague, Calfer Williams. It is either:

    a)   145/978881-89/JH.8U 067/6Y/9IU/mM54
    b)   8905-8
    c)   8905-9
    d)   8905-10

I apologise for any inconvenience, and hope you have all the information you require. In the meantime, Mr Fleckney, are you still interested in being my travelling companion on my 'Mr Nicker Nose' tour? Time is very much of the essence...

Best wishes,

Robin Cooper
Cc Calfer Williams

END OF CORRESPONDENCE

171

Robin Cooper
Brondesbury Villas
London

Mark Stanley-Price
Director
Jersey Zoo
Durrell Wildlife Conservation Trust
Les Augres Manor
Trinity
Jersey JE3 5BP

23rd March 2005

Dear Mr -Price,

I wonder if you can help.

Would it be possible for me to feed half a dozen segments of satsuma to one of your zoo's tarantulas?

Can this be arranged?

I look forward to hearing from you.

Best wishes,

Robin Cooper

DURRELL WILDLIFE
CONSERVATION TRUST
SAVING SPECIES WORLDWIDE

Mr R Cooper
Brondesbury Villas
London

Our Ref: QB/ab/directorsQB

30th March 2005

Dear Mr Cooper

Re: Tarantulas

Thank you for your letter requesting to feed Tarantulas, unfortunately we do not have any at Durrell Wildlife Conservation Trust and am therefore unable to assist.

However, I must inform you that Tarantulas do not eat fruit but insects and therefore satsumas would be an inappropriate food for them.

Yours sincerely

ff

Quentin Bloxam
Director of Zoo Programme

END OF CORRESPONDENCE

Durrell Wildlife Conservation Trust
Les Augrès Manor,
Trinity, Jersey JE3 5BP,
Channel Islands, Great Britain

Patron HRH The Princess Royal
Founder Gerald Durrell OBE LHD
Honorary Director Lee Durrell BA PhD
Executive Director Mark R Stanley Price MA DPhil

173

Robin Cooper
Brondesbury Villas
London

Imogen Stewart
Honorary Secretary
The Costume Society
c/o Moore Stephens
Warwick Lane
London EC4

24th March 2005

Dear Imogen Stewart,

I do so hope you can help (me).

In June of this year, my neighbour, Tony Sutton, is holding a party along the theme of 'Haarvantium Justice'.

I have been searching for a costume for the event but, as yet, have been unable to find anything that is suitable for the purpose.

As a leading expert on all things costumed, would you be able to offer me any assistance? For example, do you think a ruffled wristband with fluted bell-hoppers would be a good idea? I really don't know where to start.

Please help!

I look forward to hearing from you.

Best wishes,

Robin Cooper

The Costume Society

Robin Cooper
Brondesbury Villas
London

30/3/05

Dear Mr Cooper

Further to your enquiry concerning fancy dress, I am sorry but we are unable to help you. I have consulted Lindsay Evans Robertson, whom I replaced as secretary, a Dutch costume expert, a biographical dictionary and the Web. I can not find anything about Haarvantium Justice. To advise you we will need to know which period is involved.

Lindsay has very kindly offered to assist you further if you write directly to him giving more details. His address is:

Lindsay Evans Robertson
Nore Road
Portishead
North Somerset

Best wishes for your project,

Yours sincerely

Imogen Stewart
Secretary

Robin Cooper
Brondesbury Villas
London

Lindsay Evans Robertson
The Costume Society
Nore Road
Portishead
North Somerset

6th April 2005

Dear Lindsay Evans Robertson,

I believe you may have heard of my request via Imogen Stewart. I further believe that if you glance your mind's eye over the contained correspondi between myself and Imogen Stewart, you will become fully re-acquainted with my plight.

Some more details: Tony Sutton has insisted on a theme for his party (fancy dress) as 'Haarvantium Justice'. I have now been told that this is actually some form of cryptic clue as to what the theme actually is. I have therefore asked Tony Sutton for help with the unraveling (of said clue) but he will not elaborate. However he did give me the following ADDITIONAL clue....

ADDITIONAL CLUE (by Tony Sutton):

'Twinkle twinkle little car,
How I wonder whe'er you stem from,
Do not park within my capability,
My first is in 'Tea-time',
My last is in 'Coffee'.

As someone with a track record in helping others with regards to fancy dress parties, do you have any further ideas as to what the above could refer to which would point me in the right direction as to what to wear at the party?

June is fast approaching.

I thank you once again, and apologise if I have troubled you in any way.

Best wishes,

Robin Cooper

The Costume Society

Nore Road
Portishead
BRISTOL

Robin Cooper
Brondesbury Villas
LONDON

12 April 2005

Dear Mr. Cooper,

I am sorry, HAARVANTIUM JUSTICE means nothing to me, but extraordinarily, the computer spell check knows the word. Now that really is fascinating. Imogen Stewart rang me to discuss possible help and between us we have trawled where we can but without success. When you discover the meaning of the title will you please let us know? We are agog.

Initially, Imogen's call made me wonder if there is a link with people I know or knew. The name Tony Sutton rang bells, as does Brondesbury Villas, but why I have yet to fathom. Many years ago I lived in Bayswater and rattled about a lot.

A possible link may be with Werner Seehoff, in nearby Bristol, but as he is in foreign parts, either New Zealand or Australia, I can not contact him to check on this. A mutual friend thinks that this will be yet another cul-de-sac. I can only suggest that you dress in white tie and gongs and tell your host that you are a foreign ambassador to the Court of Haarvantia (but the computer spell-check thinks that I have spelt that wrongly) or decline the invitation unless he comes clean?

I enclose a membership form for our Society and hope that you will feel encouraged to take out a subscription. I also look forward to hearing how you resolve the dilemma. Perhaps Tony Sutton should take a leaf out of my book. Years ago I gave a *Greeks and Romans* party; all who arrived not in costume were offered a sheet or the door. That worked like a charm. You can have no idea how difficult it is to make a sheet look like a toga,

Yours sincerely,

Lindsay Evans Robertson (Mr.)

END OF CORRESPONDENCE

177

Brian Head
Secretary
The Crossword Club
Awbridge
Romsey
Hants
SO51 0HN

29th March 2005

Dear Mr Head,

It is an honour to write to you.

It has been a long-term ambition of mine to become a PROFESSIONAL crossword designer. What does it feel like, Mr Head?

Thus I wonder if you would take a glance at my very first attempt at designing a crossword.

In your opinion, do you feel I have what it takes to become a PROFESSIONAL crossword designer?

I thank you greatly for your time.

Respectfully yours,

I remain,

Robin Cooper

CROSSWORD PUZZLE NO. 1 (set by Robin Cooper)

ACROSS

1) Missed 'em (rhyme) (6)

5) Non-pretend electrical wall fixture (4,6)

7) Does not view interior of large primate (pidgin English) (2,3,2,3)

8) Initials (1,1,1,1)

12) Dark snake has lost his/her wallet (4,3,3)

13) Bedtime for baby's visual organ (backwards) (3,3)

DOWN

1) Non-berry eating animals (5)

2) (See 1 across) Although this answer is extended by a suffix (bit on end of word) (10)

3) Nordic god behind schedule (4,2,4)

4) Design natural water unit (4,1, gap of 1 little square, 4)

5) This bird is missing its 'w' (3)

6) Cup of golf? (3)

9) Not down (2)

10) Not in (Scottish pronunciation) (2)

11) Not, not up (2)

SOLUTION

		¹S	Y	²S	³T	E	⁴M		
		E		Y	H		A		
⁵R	E	A	L	S	O	C	K	E	⁶T
E		L		T	R		E		E
⁷N	O	S	E	E	I	N	A	P	E
			⁸E	M	S	Q			
⁹U		¹⁰O	A	L		⁶(contd). L		¹¹U
¹²P	O	O	R	T	A	N	A	S	P
		U		I	T		K		
	¹³T	O	C	E	Y	E			

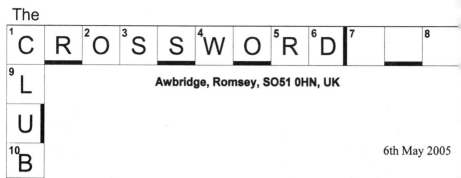

The

| C | R | O | S | S | W | O | R | D | | | |
| L |
| U |
| B |

Awbridge, Romsey, SO51 0HN, UK

6th May 2005

Dear Mr Cooper

You ask about your prospects as a professional crossword compiler. Well, alas, the marked is very crowded and there are very few indeed who make a living out of the activity; most puzzles are supplied by quite a large army of freelancers working in their spare time.

And on top of all that, your efforts do need to be suitable for their market. The use of 2-letter entries and nonwords in a diagram won't do. As a first step, I suggest you have a good look at published puzzles and study their 'rules'. If you're really keen to go ahead a good reference is Don Manley's *Chambers Crossword Manual* which is well worth reading. Computer software can be very useful for drawing and filling grids; Crossword Compiler and Sympathy are about the best programs.

I hope I haven't been too discouraging.

Best wishes

Sincerely

Brian Head

END OF CORRESPONDENCE

181

Alan Shaxon
President
The Magic Circle
Stephenson Way
London NW1

30th March 2005

Dear Mr Shaxon,

I would very much like to join your organisation. Let me rephrase that: I would like to be among the inner circle – of your Magic Circle!!!

Yes, you've probably guessed that I am a magician. Not the only one that writes to you no doubt!!!

My magician's name is 'THISPYSAURUS'. I call myself this because I go on dressed as a made-up dinosaur (Thispysaursus). My act basically combines magic for all the family with a brief lesson in Paleontology (dinosaurs).

Whilst I juggle, do card tricks and make rabbits come out of buckets, I run through the Triassic, Cretaceous and Jurassic eras, using a slide projector to illustrate my 2 hour act. The night culminates in me crushing an actual dinosaur skull with my bare hands.

Can I be a member? If not, would you allow me to tell people that I am?

With very best 'magic' wishes,

Robin Cooper

PS – I enclose an 'SAE' – a 'Spell (i.e. magic spell), Addressed Envelope!

THE MAGIC CIRCLE

Graham Reed M.I.M.C.
Examinations Secretary
Hobbs Close
St. Albans
Herts.
England

Robin Cooper Esq.,
Brondesbury Villas,
London

5th April 2005

Dear Robin,

Your letter of 30th March has been passed to me by Alan Shaxon,
the president of The Magic Circle:

We are always pleased to hear from potential members but
we are very proud of our reputation for excellence and to gain
membership it is necessary to undergo a performance examination
not exceeding twelve minutes.

The examination demands a high standard and inexperienced
performers would have problems achieving the marks necessary
for acceptance as a full Member of The Magic Circle. To determine
your suitability I suggest, Robin, you contact me by 'phone.

On a personal note I confess to being intrigued by the unusual
theme of your act - perhaps you have a video of an actual
performance.....

Best wishes,

Graham Reed MIMC
EXAMINATIONS SECRETARY - THE MAGIC CIRCLE

THE MAGIC CIRCLE
THE CENTRE FOR THE MAGIC ARTS STEPHENSON WAY LONDON NW1 2HD UK

Robin Cooper
Brondesbury Villas
London

Graham Reed M.I.M.C
Examinations Secretary
The Magic Circle
Hobbs Close
St. Albans
Herts

6th April 2005

Dear Mr Reed,

Utter thanks for your delightful letter of 5th April.

I was thrilled to learn that Alan Shaxon himself had read my words before passing them on to you. However let it be said that I am equally honoured to make your acquaintance.

You kindly asked me to call you to determine my suitability for membership. Unfortunately, I am rather incapacitated at the moment and am unable to use phones for a couple of months. I am terribly sorry but I trust you understand.

I was pleased to learn you were interested in my act. I have therefore attached a copy of one of my leaflets that audiences can refer to during my performance. I do not have a video tape at hand but I am confident that once you have read the leaflet, you will have a clear picture in you mind as to my act.

Can we now discuss membership?

I look forward to hearing from you.

Respectfully yours,

Robin Cooper

THISPYSAURUS

"IF IT'S GOOD ENOUGH FOR TYRANNOSAURUS REX, IT'S GOOD ENOUGH FOR ME!!!"

Welcome my dear spectator to the spectacle of a lifetime. For I am THISPYSAURUS, expert magician and expert paleontologist (dinosaurs).

I hope you will all sit back and enjoy my 2 hour extravaganza, featuring:

- **SLIDE SHOW:** Learn about from where these beasts of fury originated. Was it the Triassic, Cretaceous or Jurassic era? How will you score in your fun, written exam?

- **IS THIS YOUR CARD CAVEMAN/CAVEWOMAN?** Good old-fashioned card tricks, including 'Eighty Five Cards Card Trick' and 'Pillow Warfare'

- ~~**DR BRONTOSAURUS** – He's back, and he's angry! Everyone's favourite dinosaur baddie!~~ —CANCELLED

- **DINOSAUR DANCE PARTY:** Watch **THISPYSAURUS** dance the night away, blindfolded through a tunnel of knives, shaped like dinosaurs.

- **THISPYSAURUS STRONG MAN:** See **THISPYSAURUS** crush an actual dinosaur skull with his own hands.

- AND MUCH MUCH MORE...

So, what are you waiting for, let's have a big hand for...

THISPYSAURUS

...Soon to be a member of the MAGIC CIRCLE...

THE
MAGIC CIRCLE

<u>Graham Reed   M.I.M.C.</u>
Examinations Secretary
Hobbs Close
St. Albans
Herts.
England

Robin Cooper Esq.,
Brondesbury Villas,
London

11th April 2005

Dear Robin,

Thank you for your letter of 6th April:

I am sorry to learn you are currently incapacitated and trust
your problems will soon be resolved.

Unfortunately I cannot see a way we can progress your interest
in joining The Magic Circle without you contacting me by 'phone
or sending me a video of your performance. A video would be of
particular value as I would like to see Thispysaurus in action.

Can I ask you, Robin, to please remove the phrase 'Soon to be a
member of The Magic Circle' from your leaflet. We are very proud
of our name and you are assuming an outcome which may never
happen.

I suggest it would make sense if you waited, for a few weeks,
until you are fully recovered and able to use the telephone which
will enable us to discuss, in detail, your performing abilities,
and magical ambitions.

We are always pleased to hear from magical enthusiasts and it
is good to know you are keen to improve your act to ensure it
doesn't become outdated or obsolete. Dinosaurs have always had
rather a bad press and it's reassuring to learn that you are
determined to show them in a good light - as entertainers rather
than frightening killers. Keep up the good work Robin.

Best wishes,

GRAHAM (Reed)
EXAMINATIONS SECRETARY

END OF CORRESPONDENCE

THE MAGIC CIRCLE
THE CENTRE FOR THE MAGIC ARTS   STEPHENSON WAY   LONDON NW1 2HD   UK